T0339752

"Crises are progressively becoming more complex, frequent, and severe. As a result, your crisis preparedness and response capabilities must adapt to the new landscape when there is only one chance to 'get it right.' Brendan Monahan provides Crisis Management 2.0 insights that go beyond traditional preparedness and response approaches. *Strategic Corporate Crisis Management: Building an Unconquerable Organization* is a well-written and visionary guide for handling crises of the future."

Bruce T. Blythe, *Chairman R3 Continuum (Ready, Respond, Recover)*

"As a corporate security senior leader with close to 40 years of federal law enforcement, state government, and private sector security experience, I am excited to see this book from Brendan. From his time as an intelligence analyst, crisis management and business continuity professional, Brendan has developed unique insights on the emerging and complex global risk environment facing businesses today. This book will serve as a great introduction to the next generation of crisis management and business continuity leaders. It will also serve as a clear reminder to my peer/legacy security professionals on the variety, complexity, and impact from these new threats and challenges. As Brendan's book highlights, we should see such incidents/crisis as an opportunity for growth and betterment."

Edward Dickson, *Vice President, Global Security, Global Pharmaceutical Corporation*

"This book serves as a cautionary message to public and private sector managers and leaders that crises will continue to confront them, increasing in number and unfamiliarity. While public sector organizations such as fire and police departments have come to rely on the usefulness of an incident command type system and command post for managing an unfolding crisis or critical incident, it would serve them well to heed the principles and recommendations of this author. Monahan brings to the fore the criticality of public and private sector organizations being adaptive to ever-changing circumstances and situations, developing competencies among organizational personnel, and planning and preparations that should continue to evolve. It is beyond difficult, if not impossible, to plan and prepare for the type and nature of every crisis; however, the author provides thoughtful insight into how leaders and crisis team members can better serve their organizations with the goal of successful outcomes."

Russell Fischer, *Retired Chief, Miami-Dade Police Department, Miami, Florida*

STRATEGIC CORPORATE CRISIS MANAGEMENT

Presenting an alternative to traditional models of centralized crisis management, this book makes the case for decentralizing crisis response and building resilience where it matters most, and provides an accessible, pragmatic approach for doing so.

Focusing squarely on crisis management, the book challenges the notion that corporate crisis teams can be expected to swoop in and "save the day"; the role of the crisis team should be to advance a culture of readiness across an organization, and to foster leadership and crisis competency where it's needed, when it's needed. Crisis management expert Brendan Monahan draws from current management and leadership thinking that challenges hierarchies, finds incredible potential in the power of an organization's people, and aligns with many of today's highest-performing organizations that have already adopted this approach. This may run counter to current crisis management texts prescribing highly disciplined planning and command structures, but following this book's alternative approach will unlock tremendous potential, deepen resilience, and improve outcomes in crisis response.

Professionals in crisis management, business continuity, emergency management, risk management, and others with crisis management accountability will value this practical book for "corporate crisis first responders" to use when they encounter the extraordinary.

Brendan Monahan is a security intelligence and crisis professional with nearly 20 years of experience leading organizations through crisis and incident response.

STRATEGIC CORPORATE CRISIS MANAGEMENT

Building an Unconquerable Organization

Brendan Monahan

Routledge
Taylor & Francis Group
NEW YORK AND LONDON

Cover image: © Dilok Klaisataporn

First published 2023
by Routledge
605 Third Avenue, New York, NY 10158

and by Routledge
4 Park Square, Milton Park, Abingdon, Oxon, OX14 4RN

Routledge is an imprint of the Taylor & Francis Group, an informa business

Library of Congress Cataloging-in-Publication Data
Names: Monahan, Brendan, author.
Title: Strategic corporate crisis management : building the unconquerable organization / Brendan Monahan.
Description: 1 Edition. | New York, NY : Routledge, 2023. |
Includes bibliographical references and index. | .
Identifiers: LCCN 2022025250 (print) | LCCN 2022025251 (ebook) |
ISBN 9781032107387 (hardback) | ISBN 9781032107370 (paperback) |
ISBN 9781003216803 (ebook)
Subjects: LCSH: Crisis management. | Strategic planning. | Leadership. |
Corporations--Growth.
Classification: LCC HD49 .M656 2023 (print) | LCC HD49 (ebook) |
DDC 658.4/056--dc23/eng/20220728
LC record available at https://lccn.loc.gov/2022025250
LC ebook record available at https://lccn.loc.gov/2022025251

ISBN: 978-1-032-10738-7 (hbk)
ISBN: 978-1-032-10737-0 (pbk)
ISBN: 978-1-003-21680-3 (ebk)

DOI: 10.4324/9781003216803

Typeset in Joanna
by KnowledgeWorks Global Ltd.

For Elle, Finn, Lily, and Thomas

CONTENTS

AUTHOR BIOGRAPHY

Brendan Monahan is a security intelligence and crisis professional with nearly 20 years of experience in security management and crisis incident response. In that time, Brendan has guided several US companies through significant real-world crisis responses, countless incidents, and many simulations. Since 2018 he has directed the US crisis and business continuity programs for a major global pharmaceutical company, including coordinating the company's response to COVID-19 in the US. Prior to that, Brendan lead Security Resilience and Intelligence programs at two major critical infrastructure companies in the US.

He is a Steering Committee Member and recent Chair of the ASIS International Crisis Management and Business Continuity Community, and a founding member and former Chair of the New York Analyst Roundtable. Brendan is a Boston College graduate and holds an MA from Queen's University of Belfast, Northern Ireland. He also holds both the MBCI and CBCP Business Continuity Certifications, along with enhanced FEMA Incident Management and Unified Command Training.

1

PREFACE AND INTRODUCTION

Preface

Unconquerable

In his poem, Invictus, published in 1888, British poet William Ernest Henley paints a vivid picture of challenging the impenetrable darkness of a certain defeat. Some of the most powerful lines from his poem are:

> "I thank whatever Gods may be for my unconquerable soul...
> ...My head is bloody, but unbowed.
> ...The menace of the years finds and shall find me unafraid."

And most memorably,

> "I am the master of my fate. I am the captain of my soul."

DOI: 10.4324/9781003216803-1

These words have resonated through the years and been repeated by the likes of Winston Churchill and Nelson Mandela. They were recalled following the July 7, 2005 London Bombings; inspired Congressman John Lewis in his early development as a civil rights leader; and gave strength to James Stockdale during his years as a prisoner of war in North Vietnam.

Indeed, the poet Henley himself had suffered profoundly in his life. Following a severe bout of tuberculosis as a teen, his left leg had to be amputated. Some years later in the early 1870s, he experienced complications with his remaining leg and confronted the prospect of having it amputated as well. He ultimately found a surgeon who was able to save his limb. While recovering from multiple surgeries in a 19th-century Edinburgh hospital – facing the very real likelihood of gangrene, painful death or further permanent disability – Henley penned Invictus.

Many who read and celebrate Henley's words identify with his defiant tone, his will in the face of hardship and his profound stoicism. He seems powerful, indestructible, and fearless. But there is much more here.

Henley isn't just being a stoic. On the contrary, he was broken, defeated and though he says he was unafraid, I believe it is more accurate to say he was *accepting* of his fear. He was experiencing the fear, rather than simply pretending it wasn't there. In other words, he is talking about *readiness* for whatever may come – in the truest sense. The title Invictus, translates from Latin as "unconquerable."

Henley describes what it feels like to live life on life's terms, with dignity. He insists that there is greatness in the journey of living with integrity even in the worst of times, and even if no one is there to see it. This resonates strongly for me, professionally. In my career in crisis and security management I have had the tremendous opportunity to work side by side with teams of people and individual leaders who embodied the best of what is possible when circumstances seem to be at their worst. I have been able to learn by witnessing real grit and quiet determination in action.

Henley's ideas also touch me on a personal level. Like most people, at various points in life I have experienced loss, unexpected change, and disappointment. Sometimes it seems the world has plans for us other than our own. The mistake we often make is believing we are alone in confronting these situations, or that our fears are unique to us. Invictus has inspired me in those moments to pause, gain perspective, and seek the answers outside myself that I didn't want to look for. This approach hasn't failed me yet.

This book is about how to become "unconquered." Without question there is much to be gained from reflecting on these ideas as individuals. But what if we could adopt these sentiments in our organizations? What if those responsible for crisis management, and those whom they partner with, could internalize these ideas? And what if that resulted in better outcomes for workers, leaders, their organizations, and the communities that depend on them when disaster strikes?

Central to this book is the notion of becoming "unconquerable" as an enterprise, inspiring leadership from all corners – but especially on the edges and the front lines, and in the worst of times.

Introduction: into action

How can the idea of becoming unconquerable translate into better business decisions? Especially in times of crisis.

High-performing organizations confronted with crisis can choose to accept the unexpected, adopt a new normal, and bring out the best in themselves and their people. In doing so, they take a position of strength that recognizes crisis as a form of change and redefines it for a better future.

To achieve this, crisis management thinkers need to internalize two truths – born out of the lessons learned from recent global events. First, that effective crisis management does not only have to be a centralized or restricted activity. Second, crisis management thinkers have to recognize what leadership experts have known for a long time: success in a task often depends on delegating to the lowest reasonable organizational level. It turns out that responding to crises, at least to a certain extent, is no different.

There are clear advantages to taking this approach. But, more importantly, there is an obvious challenge. Namely, those on the edges of the organization – outside of the "crisis management team" – are not crisis management practitioners.

What do we do?
We can "unboss" the responders. We break down silos. And where we can't break them down, we build bridges between them.

This book delivers a practical approach for corporate crisis management teams, their partners, and stakeholders to use when they encounter the extraordinary. It will provide guidance and the tools to partner within organizations and collectively navigate the worst of times.

Can this be done while also providing the support and centralized management that a crisis situation demands?
Absolutely.

We have witnessed some organizations thrive during times of crisis, while others flounder or fail completely. It turns out that one of the keys to performing well during other-than-normal business conditions is empowering the people in an organization to rise to the challenge, rather than centralizing command and restricting control of the response.

This is especially true in large, complex organizations. Crisis leadership needs to extend to the boundaries, in the periphery – where crises are encountered. And competitive organizations – those that emerge from a crisis better than when they went in – consciously drive response activity to the fringes. But those who work at the fringes aren't crisis practitioners. They are experts in what they do – in operations, in the business. How can these workers be prepared to take part in a solution?

As an alternative to traditional models of centralized crisis management, this book makes the case for decentralizing crisis response, building resilience where it matters most, and provides an accessible, pragmatic approach for doing so. At the same time, the book will address the often-mistaken notion that corporate crisis teams can be expected to swoop in and "save the day." Rather, the role of the crisis team should be to advance a culture of readiness across an organization, fostering leadership and crisis competency where it's needed, when it's needed most.

It's this simple: Ask and answer these questions.

Who's in charge?
What needs to be done?
And, who's doing what?

The answers to these questions, in the approach presented here, form the basis of an "unconquerable" organization.

The main themes of the text will draw from current management and leadership thinking that challenges hierarchies and finds incredible potential in the power of an organization's people. As a practical matter, many of today's highest-performing organizations have already adopted this thinking. To many, this strategy may seem incongruous with crisis management texts that often prescribe highly disciplined plans and command structures. However, taking the approach presented in this book will unlock tremendous potential, deepen resilience, and improve outcomes in crisis response.

The objectives of the book will be to:

- Identify the limits of conventional crisis management approaches, while recognizing what works,
- Present the case for building "crisis competencies" throughout the organization,
- Deliver a practical approach for constructing those competencies, and
- Offer ways to think about answering the three questions: Who's in Charge, What Needs to be Done, and Who's Doing What?

What's changed

Organizations today are increasingly less hierarchical and ever more decentralized. The spectrum of risks has changed, and the level of expectation among stakeholders (regulators, customers, competitors, peers) has expanded. The world is fundamentally different from that of ten, five, or even just a few years ago. And the pace of that change is accelerating. Here are just a few examples of how the ground is shifting under our feet:

- **Integration**. More than ever before, we live in a closely integrated global economy in which specific geographical locations are less relevant, and no longer dictate when, where, and how productivity occurs. Economic and political changes appearing in the early 2000s became well established during the COVID-19 pandemic.
- **No one is safe from competition**. Thanks to technology and the global integration mentioned above, new competitors can emerge rapidly and seize the opportunity to grab market share, often before old-guard

companies can react. Common examples of this pattern are Apple's absolute dominance of the mobile phone market, or any number of online retailers that rose into prominence in the last decade (Zappos comes to mind). The proliferation of cloud computing services in the last decade meant that for dollars a month, even the smallest company could harness computing power that was unimaginable only a few years before.

- **Collaboration technologies**. Not only do people no longer have to physically be present in an office setting, but they can be virtually present in many settings globally without leaving home. This ability to collaborate across space and time drastically reduces the cost of running a global business. The experience of working remotely through COVID has provided many businesses and individuals who had previously shunned the idea of remote work with valuable lessons on what is possible. As well, this has shown effectively what some of the limits of virtual collaboration are – and when or how real world interaction is most meaningful. In a world where workers are less engaged in routine tasks and more devoted to knowledge based tasks, striking the right balance of collaboration is a key factor in succeeding.

- **Values and Personal Brand**. More than in any previous generation, today's workers are likely to value their own professional and personal identity over allegiance to their employer. Whereas once upon a time an employer could dictate much about an individual's life and professional development, today's workers have far more independence and have shown a tendency to favor employers who respect – or even embody – their personal values. The organizations that can do this well will draw in and retain the best talent. And that talent will stay because they want to, not because they have to. This is a competitive advantage to both the employer and the employee.

- **New Patterns of Risk**. Emerging risks are manifesting in new and unexpected ways, leading to the occurrence of crises with greater frequency and regularity. For this reason, existing patterns of response and plan templates can fall short. There is also greater complexity among the crises that today's companies experience. Familiar threats from the outside of organizations such as natural disasters, severe weather, security incidents (like active shooter situations and terrorist threats) continue. At the same time, new threats emerge from within companies (such as technology or operational failures; misconduct; and deliberate or accidental product failures) which can be much harder to detect early or respond to holistically.

Traditional management concepts are changing to keep up with these new patterns. It is already clear that organizations that do not adapt well to these changes will fail to compete and cease to exist. Consequently, it seems clear that approaches to managing crises should also be reviewed as present systems may no longer be relevant. The response to the 2020 COVID19 outbreak puts a very fine point on this topic.

In fact, a more diversified approach may result in organizations finding opportunity in crisis, rather than mere survival.

In March 2021, PwC's Global Crisis Survey collected feedback from more than 2,800 global business leaders across dozens of countries and industries. The survey found that more than 30% of respondents did not have a designated core crisis team in place at the start of the COVID-19 pandemic. Not surprisingly, nearly all respondents (up to 95%) reported that their crisis management capabilities needed improvement. What is most telling about the PwC data is the fact that only 20% of organizations surveyed reported that the pandemic had an overall positive effect on their business. Clearly much of that 20% is sector driven – most likely by life sciences brands, pharmaceutical companies, and services that benefit from the changes brought by the pandemic.

This seems like a missed opportunity. To be clear, companies should never seek to profit from or take advantage of crisis for commercial gain. The truth is that crisis is a form of change – and properly harnessed that change can bring about powerful improvements and raise prospects not only for the organization experiencing the crisis, but for communities as a whole. The question becomes how this can be done, and what role can corporate crisis teams play?

―――――――――――――――――――

Thinking ahead toward a culture of readiness

Part of the answer to the question lies in corporate culture. It is not unusual for corporate cultures to be restrictive, brittle, and far less adaptive than their public personas may imply. Fortunately, some of that has started to change.

In their 2012 book, *Unboss*, authors Lars Kolind and Jacob Botter argue that many organizations, of various sizes and across industries, are failing to compete because they apply management practices that are obsolete.

Their ambition was to upend the conventional hierarchy of bosses and direct reports and the associated bureaucracy found in modern organizations. Instead, they propose the "unboss" – which is the opposite of a boss. A person who acts as a leader, but in a "...radically different way to the managers we know today."[1]

Kolind and Botter offer comparisons among the standards, values, and behaviors characteristic of "bosses" and those of "Unbosses."[2]

- Whereas a "boss" may be "motivated by profit, generates a financial return based on the budget and planned production," an "Unboss," is "...motivated by a purpose, creates meaning and value based on common purpose."[3]
- Where a "boss" is superior, an "unboss" is a partner or teammate.[4]
- "Bosses" control, direct, and talk; "Unbosses" inspire, serve and listen.[5]
- The traditional "boss" will analyze, plan, execute and control. Whereas, the "unboss" instead inspires, focuses, encourages and acknowledges.[6]

In other words, Unbossed leaders take responsibility and hold others to account for their behavior. They create clarity, set direction and boundaries, and help people understand what they are accountable for – and what they are not. Leaders in this context are judged by their ability to remove barriers (rather than create them); and by their ability to empower and support those around them.

At the organizational level, summarized most succinctly, Unboss consists of three components:

"The UNBOSS organization involves **everybody instead of the few**, it functions through **mechanisms instead of structures**, and it builds on **purpose instead of profit**."[7]

Do well by doing good: living companies and "unbossing" crisis management

What does any of this have to do with crisis management?

In a conventional setting, crisis management is a specialist task – and appropriately so. There are without a doubt highly specific skills and talents required to perform well in a crisis management role. And very often these skills are gathered together and centralized in a large company, a practice which makes good business sense in most cases.

But it is also worth remembering that crisis management is pain management, and pain management is a dangerous way to manage through change.[8] Crisis management is also – often by necessity – autocratic. This means that it can be very effective at delivering fast decision making, but it is also the case that implementation of those decisions with speed can come at the expense of quality.[9] Or perhaps with their own risks.

An unbossed approach advocates for involving other specialists in the process, bringing the right experts to the table at the right time, and leveraging the collective wisdom of the organization.

Consider the elements of *Unboss* above in the context of a crisis team.

- **Everyone instead of the few**. The crisis team should take the shape of its container – not be confined to a small, predetermined team. Build a brand around a crisis response that includes the "many."
- **Mechanism vs structure**. Anything with moving parts is a mechanism; things that can only move as a whole are structures. When crisis strikes, the team should guide the response but not direct every aspect of it. Where needed and appropriate, parts and pieces should be able to move independently of the whole while keeping the entire organization moving toward the common goal.
- **Purpose instead of profit**. Being purposeful always matters, but never more so than when things are at their seeming worst. Acting with integrity and being transparent may not always improve the bottom line. But in today's world it bears repeating that businesses can't survive in societies that fail.

The ideas presented in *Unboss* are helpful in framing up a conversation. At the same time, the observations contained in the book are not as revolutionary as they may appear. In the 1980s and 1990s, Dutch business strategist Arie de Geus in the Strategic Planning Group at Royal Dutch Shell was already leading detailed studies of why some companies survive generations – even centuries – navigating successfully through multiple crises. His analysis looked at an inventory of 30 companies who had remained in business for between 100 and 700 years, the so-called "Living Companies." This includes Japan's Sumimoto, founded in 1590, and Swedish company Stora Enso whose origins date back to 1590.

What can be learned from companies that survived every global conflict since gunpowder was invented, stayed viable through every industrial revolution, and even managed through bubonic plague pandemics in the middle ages? It turns out, quite a lot can be learned.

According to de Geus, living companies teach us the following:[10]

- Organizations die because they forget they are a community of human beings.
- Organizations survive when they value people, not assets.
- Managers in living companies allow loosening of steering and control.
- Living companies are organized for learning.
- They take a role in shaping their human community at large.

There are a lot of great books on crisis management out there. On the one hand, a lot of very high-quality academic research on the subject brings together great minds from across many fields and has significantly advanced the theoretical framework for this discipline. There are also quite a few very good textbooks and procedural texts that can be used as reference material for those of us in the field. Many outstanding books on the subject also closely examine case studies to draw out lessons; while others convey the lived experience of practitioners who have experienced and led crisis teams firsthand.

While I have been in the crisis and security management field for many years as a practitioner in the public and private sectors, this book is not about my story. Nor does this book present a unified theory of crisis management. It is also not intended to be a retelling of case studies in search of best practices or lessons learned, although I do refer to real examples from the public domain of crises to illustrate points.

Instead, this book is an invitation to look at crisis differently. Many of the books on this subject emphasize the planning and preparation phases of crisis management – this one does as well, but I also focus on the limits of planning and how we should shape responses in progress. Much of the writing in this field also prescribes individual behaviors or characteristics that people managing crises should embody. The approach presented here, however, emphasizes organizing for response and building broad competencies across disciplines in the organization.

My hope is to provoke the reader to reflect on their own experiences and bring those experiences to bear on the work of crisis management in a way that breaks from traditional, strict approaches. I hope to share an open-minded approach to doing crisis management in a way that may be more in line with today's crises, but also more aligned to the culture of today's businesses and workers. These ideas won't be for everyone and won't be a fit in every organization. But I invite crisis practitioners, their partners, stakeholders, and clients to give some consideration to what follows. The challenge is to imagine what crisis response can look like with loosened control, and more direct involvement with the edges of the organization.

This book is divided into three parts. The first part looks at the context of current and past crisis management practices with an eye toward an alternative that may better serve crisis management practitioners, their partners, and stakeholders. The second part presents the core elements of what I believe to be a pragmatic solution to the gaps in traditional practice. Lastly, the third part presents what I believe to be the most important questions (and answers) in any crisis management response: Who's in charge, What needs to be done, and Who's doing what?

There is a logical order to these parts, but there is no reason to necessarily read this book from start to end in a linear fashion. My hope is that the reader can open to any section of this book and find something that resonates, or something to refer to when needed. At times you may be curious about crisis leadership, and at other times more focused on teams or why we often do things a certain way in crisis management. At any stage of this book, I hope you will find material that prompts questions and ideas in your mind about how things can be done better or differently in your own organization.

TAKEAWAY

The intent of this book is to offer tools and a framework for thinking differently about crisis management – what it means to practitioners, leaders, customers, regulators, and those on the front lines who may find themselves thrust into an unexpected, unimaginable situation.

Who's in Charge, What Needs to be Done, and Who's Doing What?

If you can stop the action long enough to ask and answer those questions, you are beginning to manage crisis and lead toward stability. If you either cannot stop the action, or you cannot answer these questions, the situation will remain unstable.

If an organization can succeed in doing this with dignity and the intent to do the next right thing – or better yet – if it can *program* to do so, then it is building an *Unconquerable* organization.

Notes

1. Lars Kolind and Jacob Botter, *Unboss* (Jyllands-Postens Forlag), 1st edition, October 1, 2012, p. 5.
2. Ibid, p. 37.
3. Ibid.
4. Ibid.
5. Ibid.
6. Ibid.
7. *Unboss Summary* pdf – p. 4. (http://efnet.si/wp-content/uploads/Lars-Kolind-book-Unboss.pdf)
8. Arie de Gues, "Planning As Learning," *Harvard Business Review Magazine* March 1988.
9. Ibid.
10. Arie de Gues, "The Living Company," *Harvard Business Review Magazine* March–April 1997.

PART I

2

OLD IDEAS BECOME
NEW AGAIN

What's the plan vs
what's the story?

Overview

This chapter reflects on the gap between planning and true readiness
and challenges the notion that planning alone is equivalent to readiness.
Without discounting the value and importance of a solid planning process,
it is also the case that the reality of the situation often does not meet the
expectations of the plan. There are some helpful academic thought models on crisis that inform a view on this tension between planning and
response – as well as some practical steps that effective teams have shown
are successful. The truth that most crisis management practitioners already
know is that you do not come out of a crisis the same way you went in.
There is a story that takes place in every crisis, with a beginning or opening, a middle or rising action, and some kind of resolution. Sometimes the
story repeats or continues into a new chapter, and sometimes it concludes.
Either way, the unfolding crisis makes everyone a part of the story it tells.
Knowing and accepting that truth enables the team to think in terms of the
story rather than just the plan.

DOI: 10.4324/9781003216803-3

The von Moltke theory of war

Born in northern Germany in October 1800, Helmuth Karl Bernhard Graf von Moltke – better known as "Von Moltke the Elder" – was a senior Prussian Army Official and a highly regarded military strategist. He commanded armies in Europe and the Middle East during the Second Schleswig War, Austro-Prussian War, and the Franco-Prussian War. He is most often noted for his pioneering approach to military command in response to rapidly changing technological and tactical conditions at the time.

As he once said,

> Victory or defeat in battle changes the situation to such a degree that no human acumen is able to see beyond the first battle. Therefore, no plan of operation extends with any certainty beyond the first contact with the main hostile force... The advantage of the situation will never be fully utilized if subordinate commanders wait for orders, it will be generally more advisable to proceed actively and keep the initiative than to wait to the law of the opponent.

This quote, summarized as "no plan of operation extends with any certainty beyond the first contact with the main hostile force," or "no plan survives first contact with the enemy" is well understood by crisis management practitioners. It has been reconfigured in many ways over the years since Von Moltke commanded armies – but the concept remains as true today as it was then.

The Von Moltke theory of war rests on the idea that military strategy must be understood as a system of options and accepts that it is only possible to plan the beginning of a military operation. Once the battle begins, external factors beyond the players' control immediately begin acting against the assumptions inherent in any plan. In today's language, we would say those factors are best described as the loss of knowability and the increase in uncertainty.

How did von Moltke arrive at this theory? Following several significant military defeats in the early 1800s, Prussian General Staff began a review of their field service regulations. One of the key findings of their review was that "...the French achieved high tempo through rapid communication of Napoleon's intentions and rationale. Perhaps most important, the exercise of initiative by junior officers was tolerated … the result was an operational tempo which left the incredulous Prussians bewildered."[1]

The Prussian military's analysis concluded – correctly – that they had been outrun and overpowered not because of Napoleon's superior command abilities or leadership, and not because of better discipline on the part of French forces. Rather, their opposing French junior leadership – on an individual basis – clearly understood the purpose and intent of their commander so well that they were able to respond actively to the specific conditions they faced in their areas of the battlefield, while remaining aligned to that intent. Even when separated from the direct lines of command and control from their leadership, these junior officers were evidently capable of acting coherently – even independently – toward their common objective.

The approach favored flexibility over rigidity; it rewarded initiative over obedience; and allowed for action to occur where orders could not flow. The Prussians could not argue with the outcome. They adopted the notion into their own field service manuals, "if an execution of an order was rendered impossible, an officer should seek to act in line with the intention behind it."[2] Officers were expected to exercise judgement and "mistakes were preferable to hesitancy to enable decisive bold action."[3]

This approach was counter to the prevailing wisdom of the time, particularly among Prussian military leadership, who had traditionally favored systems of rules, dictated to highly regimented and disciplined ranks – whose input on their superiors' tactics was not necessarily welcome.

Von Moltke, and other strategists such as Carl von Clausewitz, saw military strategy instead as the art of adapting means to ends in changing times. In the 1790s and early 1800s, centralized command control of armies could be effectively managed, as was the case with Napoleon and Wellington.

However, rapid improvements in basic infrastructure across the Continent saw widespread construction of roads, railways, and canals allowing people and materials to move far more efficiently over greater distances than ever before. This occurred at the same time as the adoption of new communications technology – such as the telegraph – and advancements in cartography and mapping capabilities which enabled military coordination to occur with far greater precision and accuracy.

By the 1820s armies had also grown significantly in size, to the extent that exercising detailed command over the entire force simultaneously was no longer possible. This meant, to von Moltke, that in order for forces to become manageable they had to be broken into smaller contingent parts – each of which could be authorized to act with some autonomy within a broader set of executive principles. As long as units understood the purpose and direction of the overall operation, they could be free to make localized decisions as the flow of battle necessitated.

What were the core elements of von Moltke's new approach?

- Junior Officers should be empowered by their leaders to act independently in order to be effective in battle.
- They should be trained to develop initiative and practice good judgment within the guardrails of their commanders' intent.
- Junior Officers should be required to exercise their initiative in the absence of direct orders.
- The decentralized approach to war should be exercised as an advantage whenever possible.

To achieve this, commanders would need to state intentions – rather than specific orders – and be willing to accept reasonable deviations within the overall framework. In other words, building consensus around the broad mission goals matters more than delivering specific, detailed direction.

A simple illustration of this concept is as follows. A commander's direct order to a small unit could be to "cross the bridge and capture the town." When the unit arrives at the bridge and discovers the crossing has been blown up by the enemy, they proceed no further in the absence of direct orders. The unit is now stranded and vulnerable, and no longer contributing to the overall mission.

However, in von Moltke's new imagining, the commander's intent is articulated as "capture the town to support the westward advance our supply line." The unit deploys to the bridge and finds it has been blown up by the enemy. Without further direction, they then proceed upriver to a shallow crossing, cross the water, connect back to the road, and capture the town. In this variation, the unit understands the bigger picture – and is empowered to define the means to the end.

In its simplest terms, von Moltke's theory on war can be understood as a system of options, in which the only thing it is possible to plan is the opening move of a military operation. In many ways, what he describes

sounds a lot like modern-day concepts of empowering teams and individuals, loosening of controls, inspiring principled leadership, and driving accountability to lower levels in the organization. Following from this
premise, von Moltke held that a primary task of military leaders should be
the detailed preparation for all possible outcomes. But therein lies what
may be a critical pitfall.

If no plan survives first contact with the enemy, is the only logical solution, then, to plan for every imaginable threat? It turns out that may not
be a valuable exercise. In fact, that may not be a practical benefit at all. Is
it possible that contemporary crisis management planning has returned to
some of the mistakes of the past?

Crisis management thought models

When thinking about the practical world of crisis management – especially
for those who don't reflect on these topics every day – two quotes stand
out:

> The first is commonly attributed to Mike Tyson. "Everyone has a
> plan until they get punched in the face."
>   The other has been attributed to Mike Hillmann, former LAPD
> Deputy Chief and a well-known incident management expert. "Not
> every incident has a playbook – sometimes you just have to think!"[4]

What is compelling and most relevant about each of these comments is
what they seem to say about the role of planning and preparation in confrontation with the unexpected. There can be a tendency in the crisis management, emergency response, and business continuity worlds to invest
tremendous time and energy on elaborate, often highly detailed and specific plans. It is also common practice among these communities in the
course of revising such plans to criticize one another for "preparing to fight
the last war."

Neither Tyson nor Hillmann was an entirely uncontroversial figure at
the height of his game. But they spoke their minds and what they most
definitely got right here was the notion that 1) preparation alone does not
equal readiness; and 2) the unexpected will always occur, but that does not
excuse poor execution or response.

In other words, Mike Tyson wasn't suggesting that he didn't train and prepare for a big fight. On the contrary, he had access to the best trainers and preparation in the world and brought tremendous discipline and dedication to his regimen. But he also had the wisdom to acknowledge a truth about the world he lived in. That when the bell rings and the moment comes, the reality of that situation may not resemble one's expectations. Even worse, at the point of impact that readiness may well evaporate. In which case, what do you do?

Here is where Hillmann steps in, resolving the planning and action tension with a simple command, "just think!" The solution isn't having plans and playbooks perfectly tailored to every imaginable risk readily available to the crisis team. Nor is it finding the right playbook to match whatever unfolding incident is taking place. It may be an instinctive approach to managing a crisis to define the *answer* to the problem as fast as possible. Instead – as Hillmann implies – the solution lies in defining the *question*. And to do that... just think.

The more academic term for this approach, introduced by organizational theorist Karl Weick, is "sensemaking." The term refers to "how we structure the unknown so as to be able to act in it... coming up with a plausible understanding – a map – of a shifting world."[5]

Or as Weick said himself, sensemaking is literally just what it says it is: making sense.

There is a fair amount of academic and business research on this topic. However, many of today's crisis management practices are also derived from military, law enforcement and public sector sources, with good reason. As a practical matter, many law enforcement, military personnel, and first responders spend a great deal of time training and preparing to respond to specific events: fires, traffic accidents, common attack vectors, or even things like active shooter incidents.

But what of the incidents that defy these common patterns? And what about those who may find themselves responding to a crisis in a private sector setting – those who are not trained first responders, but who instead have a primarily operational role in a business?

In those cases, the common approaches may be losing relevance. Or are being challenged by increasingly complex, but less hierarchical organizations which are confronted with new kinds of risks in a new business environment.

Arriving at a workable solution calls for a critical analysis to determine what works, what doesn't and – in the subsequent chapters – what other solutions are available.

What does good look like?

If we take von Moltke, Hillman, and Mike Tyson at their words and reflect on the possibility that perfect planning does not equate to perfect readiness, what does good look like when we are confronted with a situation that defies our best planning?

An interesting example of this emerges from the performance of air traffic controllers at Anchorage, Alaska airport following back-to-back earthquakes on November 30, 2018.

On that morning, at 8:29 AM, a magnitude 7.1 earthquake rocked Anchorage, followed by a second 5.8 magnitude quake shortly thereafter. The quakes were centered about seven miles north of the city and prompted people to run from homes and offices, take cover under desks, and flee to higher ground following an accompanying tsunami warning for the area. While human costs and loss of life were not widespread, the damage in the area was extensive – with buckled roadways and damage to buildings and property.

In the air traffic control tower, 150 feet above the runways at Ted Stevens Anchorage International Airport (ANC), air traffic controllers were forced into action. ANC is one of the world's busiest for air cargo and is a hub for a number of commercial passenger and cargo carriers, including FedEx, UPS, Alaska Airlines, and Atlas Air.

At the moment the initial quake struck that morning, a FedEx cargo jet was on final approach about 300–400 feet above the runway and about to land. Not knowing the extent of damage to the runways, air traffic controllers screamed over the radio for the jet to abort the landing, pull up and go around the airport. Dramatic radio transmissions from that moment depict an air traffic controller trying to reach the pilot: "FedEx Heavy, Go Around! FedEx Heavy go around!" What follows can be heard in recordings of radio transmissions from the day and is truly fascinating.

It is worth noting that this wasn't ANC Airport's first experience of this kind. In 1964, the "Good Friday Earthquake" struck the area and collapsed the ANC control tower, killing George Taylor, the FAA Air Traffic Controller on duty in the tower at the time.

Knowing this had happened before makes the response of the airport workers in 2018 even more admirable – especially those that stayed behind in the damaged control tower until it could be evacuated. It also meant that the airport had a plan for such situations and had most likely exercised it. There was a period of time in which the controllers had to transition to a backup communications protocol – known as CTAF – whereby aircraft in the area radioed their position and heading to one another while the tower operation was temporarily offline.

In the event that the control tower became damaged or inaccessible for whatever reason, Plan B was to relocate to the airport fire station. On this particular day, however, that location turned out to be inaccessible too. Plan B was no longer on the table.

What ensued was not a scenario where the hypothetical commander's soldiers stop at the blown-up bridge and await further orders indefinitely. Rather, this team quickly improvised a solution, managed to continue safely landing aircraft, and saw almost no interruption to airport operations. And that solution was quite simply, air traffic controllers with binoculars and radios in the bed of a Ford F-150 parked on the runway. In the span of minutes, the team had to transition from their normal operating conditions to completely extraordinary ones. In doing so, they managed the air traffic without interruption, coordinated with airport operations on the status of their runways, responded to inquiries from outside stakeholders (such as medevac aircraft seeking permission to take off), determined that their backup plan was inoperable, and quickly improvised a new one.

In looking at this from a crisis management practitioner's standpoint, several things stand out.

Quickly identify the triggering event

First, the team on the ground very quickly identified the "triggering event." In other words, the team immediately recognized that something unexpected was happening, and that it required immediate action on their part.

This may sound obvious – especially in the case of an earthquake. But it is far less obvious, and far more important to effective crisis management, than it may seem. As an example, in August 2011, a 5.8 magnitude earthquake in central Virginia shook buildings in Northern New Jersey and the Greater New York City region. For residents of New Jersey, earthquakes are exceptionally rare, and most have never experienced one. In fact, on that morning in 2011 – only about half of the people in any given building even felt the quake. Some experienced slight shaking and a mild dizzy sensation, some experienced panic, and some experienced... nothing at all. There was no damage to speak of, and no loss of life. But the response to the event on the part of a population largely unfamiliar with the phenomenon was striking. Many self-evacuated glass-curtain office buildings (against their building management's guidance), only to stop at the outside and stare directly up at the swaying glass building above them. This is seemingly non-sensical behavior to, say, a resident of California who experiences tremors like this on a regular basis.

The point is, if a team can identify what is happening quickly, they are less likely to be overtaken by events. In business operations, or in security threat scenarios, defining the "triggering event" can often be very challenging because of the complexity or speed with which the action occurs. In the case of the Alaskan air traffic control team, they benefited from quickly stepping into action when they recognized what was happening.

Focus on initial objectives

Upon recognizing that an earthquake had occurred, and would require action on their part, the team did not immediately refer to their *Earthquake Response Playbook*. Judging from the audio, it is apparent that they quickly focused around initial objectives. Namely, air traffic safety ("FedEx Heavy Go Around!"); Continuity of communications (transitioning to their CTAF protocol so that aircraft in the area could maintain awareness and communications with one another); and the safe evacuation of their damaged control tower.

This focus on the critical things that matter meant that the team was able to adapt to the changing conditions around them. While their earthquake plan did anticipate damage to the control tower, it did not specify what to do when the backup location was compromised. And even if it had clearly defined what to do in that eventuality, that Plan C could just as easily have been rendered useless by the same circumstances. Having a plan gave them an advantage, helped them make sense of what was happening, and created some options. But having a team focused on initial objectives gave them flexibility. As one of the controllers that day remarked, "Most of our equipment is windows. We had a window in the truck," referring to the pickup truck that was driven out onto the tarmac as a makeshift control tower. "Everybody had a radio. Everybody had a phone."[6]

Appropriately address stakeholders

That flexibility allowed the team to respond better to the changing conditions and be open to an improvised solution. Remarkably, in the midst of everything that was going on, the team also managed to remain accessible to stakeholders – airport operations communicating status; runway inspectors reporting updates; inbound air traffic; and medevac aircraft. Some of these stakeholders were essential, but some were more essential than others. In the early stages of a crisis, it can often be difficult to determine the difference and prioritize – especially when all of the agencies feel their needs are most important.

Having quickly recognized the triggering event and established rough early objectives means that the situation is beginning to make sense. Once the team achieves that degree of comprehension, it becomes easier to address stakeholders.

Uncertainty and knowability

The team managed through a highly acute situation with no significant impact on airport operations. "Obviously, there are rules and you're supposed to follow them, so you'd never say you're supposed to be super creative," Sherri LaRue, associate professor of aviation technology at University of Alaska Anchorage said. "But not everything is covered by a rule."[7]

In Anchorage that day, this acknowledgment was key to their ultimate success. Not every context was covered by a rule; their plan got "punched in the face;" they had to think their way through without a playbook; and their plans sufficed until the situation started acting against them.

These realities show how in any crisis situation the forces of uncertainty and knowability are acting on all of the players. The action of these forces is also the reason why planning alone is not always sufficient. The teams and organizations that prevail when things are at their worst are able to grapple with these forces and turn the tide.

The story of the air traffic controllers in Anchorage that day reflects some of the best practices of effective teams in crisis. It is an example of how a small and highly effective team can perform superbly, under extraordinary circumstances. How do we adapt their responses for larger, highly complex, global enterprises? How do we apply this strategy where – perhaps – to the outside observer– what's at stake is not so obviously of a life-and-death nature? Can other organizations, that serve our communities every day, and on whom we depend or whose products are of critical value to a small, highly dependent community or customer group develop similar approaches to crises?

Crisis defined

The word "crisis" is derived from the Latinized form of the Greek word *krisis*, which can mean "moment of decision" or "turning point."

By contrast, the etymology of the word "disaster" originates from Latin and Italian terms meaning "ill-starred event" or "bad alignment of stars."

Implicit in the root word of *crisis* is the notion of taking action and bringing about change.

A crisis is a confrontation, a call to action – it brings players into the conflict. On the other hand, "disaster" understood as a "bad alignment of stars" renders one powerless. There is no role for us to take against a bad alignment of stars other than that of a victim, because in a literal sense there is nothing we can do to influence the movement of heavenly bodies. It is by definition beyond the reach of our control.

But the word *crisis* presents us with a challenge and an opportunity. The crisis may truly be a situation which is abnormal, extraordinary, or highly threatening to an organization. Inherent in the meaning of the word, however, is the requirement to act – and to do so in a way that is strategic and adaptive or flexible. The *crisis* may exceed the ability of an organization to respond – or stretch its resources to the brink. But it also invites the organization to respond in a dynamic way that might never have been exercised or anticipated.

The implication, therefore, is that something powerfully unexpected is taking place and we are called upon not only to address it and cope with it, but also somehow to participate in it as story that is unfolding before us.

OTHER DEFINITIONS OF CRISIS

"Any emotionally charged situation that, once it becomes public, invites negative stakeholder reaction and thereby has the potential to threaten the financial wellbeing, reputation or survival of the firm or some portion thereof."

- Erica Hayes James and Lynn Perry Wooten, "Leadership as (Un)usual: How to Display Competence in Times of Crisis," Organizational Dynamics 34, no. 2 (2005): 142.

"A low-probability, high-impact event that threatens the viability of the organization and is characterized by ambiguity of cause, effect, and means of resolution, as well as by a belief that decisions must be made swiftly."

- Christine M. Pearson and Judith A. Clair, "Reframing Crisis Management," Academy of Management Review 23 (1998): 60.

"...a serious threat to the basic structure or the fundamental values and norms of a social system, which – under time pressure and highly uncertain circumstances – necessitates making critical decisions."

- Uriel Rosenthal, Paul 't Hart, and Michael T. Charles, "The World of Crises and Crisis Management," in Coping with Crises: The Management of Disasters, Riots and Terrorism, ed.

"...a situation that threatens high-priority goals of the decision-making unit, restricts the amount of time available for response before the decision is transformed and surprises the members of the decision-making unit by its occurrence."

- C. F. Hermann, International Crises: Insights from Behavioral Research (New York: Free Press, 1972), as quoted in Uriel Rosenthal and Alexander Kouzmin, "Crises and Crisis Management: Toward Comprehensive Government Decision Marking," Journal of Public Administration Research and Theory 7, no. 2 (1997): 279.

Models of crisis – tell the crisis story

There are numerous models of crisis delineated in the academic literature on crisis management. Some follow 3-stage models, others 4-stages. Some have six steps and others take the four-cluster approach.

Models such as Fink's (1986) Four Stage Model pattern after the disease analogy, whereby crisis moves like an illness through a patient from pro-dromal or pre-symptomatic to acute to chronic and then on to resolution. This approach is sometimes criticized for failing to acknowledge the cyclical or iterative nature of crises.

Ian Mitroff built upon these ideas when he introduced a five-stage model in 1994 which included 1) signal detection, 2) probing and prevention, 3) containment, 4) recovery, and 5) learning. Mitroff is credited as being among the first to note that preparing for every imaginable threat is not beneficial. Instead, Mitroff proposed that while no two crises are the same, they often share common characteristics. Consequently, crises could be grouped into categories or "clusters" with like features. The crisis team could then apply a broad crisis plan or portfolio of plans to many incidents within a cluster, without the need to create innumerable plans to cover each risk. He proposed a similar approach to preventative measures.

The Gonzelez-Herroro and Pratt model aligned with the Mitroff approach, but the articulated crisis in terms of a lifecycle of birth, growth, maturity, and decline. The role of the crisis management team in this construct is to limit the duration of the crisis lifecycle, and prevent it from propagating further crises.

There are many other models – and fierce academic debate – concerning their relative merits. An analysis of that debate is outside the scope of this work. But it is important to acknowledge their presence insofar as the leading models do share some broadly common characteristics. Namely – there is a notion contained within each of these models of linearity or of the cyclical nature of the crisis. Some prefer a linear approach, others a cycle. Regardless of which approach is correct – inherent in these models is the existence of a beginning, a middle, and some kind of end or resolution. A pattern of escalation and de-escalation exists in every crisis.

Quite simply, and in other words, there is a story being told. We recognize that in confrontation with a crisis — whatever the specifics are — we will come out the other side different, or transformed, as a result of the experience. The Greek krisis makes us part of the story and demands our involvement.

Von Moltke's ideas were probably not at the forefront of the minds of those Air Traffic controllers at Anchorage Airport that day. More than likely, they have never heard of him. But their actions embodied the strengths of what he intended. The question is how to program for this on a larger scale and win the support of many in large enterprises, especially when the plans fail to meet the needs of the crisis. In those cases, how do we tell the story and drive action to better outcomes?

From this perspective, it is the duty of the crisis team to recognize that unfolding narrative and respond to it. The crisis team, its stakeholders, the organization, and those involved with it will have to take hold of the crisis and bring action to bear, driving from the edges and adapting. In doing so, they become part of the action and influence the telling of the story in progress. This is central to the idea of *sensemaking*. Karl Weick described *sensemaking* in the context of crisis as "being thrown into an ongoing, unknowable, unpredictable streaming of experience in search of answers to the question, 'What's the story?'"

That requires the ability to quickly identify that something is happening — an incident is underway. A team must then get some initial goals or objectives sorted out; clarify who the stakeholders are and what matters to them; and take appropriate action despite the forces of uncertainty and knowability acting against the crisis team. What, then, does leadership in this context require? How do we structure the response and connect decision-making to operations?

To be clear, by "story" I am not referring to media spin or communicating a narrative to the public. What is meant here is totally different. It is a reflection of the crisis models in which there are beginnings or triggering events, followed by subsequent developments, leading to the next chapters or resolution of the crisis.

Having a plan is prudent; essential even. But planning alone is not the same as readiness. Being willing and able to engage and define the "story" in progress will always result in better outcomes. This idea isn't new.

TAKEAWAY

- No Plan Survives the First Shot. Rather than innumerable threat-specific plans, prepare to develop a system of options in response to likely outcomes, and funnel them down as conditions dictate.
- Delegate to the lowest reasonable levels for maximum flexibility and speed.
- Small teams can do this with great effectiveness. But larger organizations can also program crisis response for speed and flexibility. Those that do it best do the following:
  - o Recognize triggering events quickly,
  - o Focus on initial objectives and practice iterative leadership,
  - o Always appropriately address stakeholders, and above all
  - o Accept the unknowability and uncertainty of their circumstances.
- Crisis doesn't just happen to you – it forces you into action and requires choices.
- Effective crisis responses reflect a recognition of and – eventually – a mastery over the *story* the crisis is trying to tell with the circumstances it is presenting. Effective crisis responses influence that story with the choices they make.

Notes

1. Keith G. Stewart, "The Evolution of Command Approach" (Paper 192), paper presented at the International Command and Control Research and Technology Symposium, Santa Monica, Calif., June 2010, p. 4.
2. Ivan Yardley and Andrew Kakabadse, "Understanding Mission Command: A Model for Developing Competitive Advantage in a Business Context," Strategic Change, Vol. 16, No. 1–2, January–April 2007, pp. 69–78.
3. Stewart, p. 6.
4. As cited by Cynthia Renaud, "The Missing Piece of NIMS: Teaching Incident Commanders How to Function in the Edge of Chaos." Homeland Security Affairs, Volume 8, Article 8, June 2012, p. 8.
5. Deborah Ancona, "Sensemaking: Framing and Acting in the Unknown," The Handbook for Teaching Leadership, Chapter 1, p. 3.
6. https://www.alaskapublic.org/2018/12/04/post-earthquake-air-traffic-controllers-exiled-from-anchorage-tower-used-a-pickup-truck-instead/
7. https://www.alaskapublic.org/2018/12/04/post-earthquake-air-traffic-controllers-exiled-from-anchorage-tower-used-a-pickup-truck-instead/

3

THE PROBLEM, THE CHALLENGE, AND A SOLUTION

The problem

Organizations confronted with a crisis can emerge stronger and experience crisis as a form of growth. Pragmatic ways to achieve this growth may be rooted in best practices, but also require new thinking.

Beginning from the premise that planning alone is not equivalent to readiness, there are clear roles and responsibilities outside of planning activity that must come into play both in responses to crises – and in the periods of time when we are "preparing."

If that's the case, then it stands to reason that crisis management need not be only a centralized activity. Experience shows that the bad things that happen to organizations occur, or can be detected earliest, at the operational edges of the business.

Some questions come to mind:

- What is the best way to connect those at the edges to the crisis management team or process at the center?

DOI: 10.4324/9781003216803-4

- How do we proceed to "tell the story" of the unfolding crisis – especially in a highly integrated or complex organization?
- How do we scale up from a small, highly flexible team capable of feats of impressive agility to pivoting on a larger scale? Especially in times when the plan doesn't align with the circumstances?

There are already good, practical approaches in use. How well do they answer these questions – and what gaps remain?

To ICS or not to ICS: the limits of ICS for private companies

The Incident Command System (ICS) is a standardized, centralized approach to "… the command, control, and coordination of on-scene incident management, providing a common hierarchy within which personnel from multiple organizations can be effective."[1]

In the post-9/11 world, ICS is ubiquitous in responses across public and private sector incidents – and is commonly referred to as a need or gap in contemporary after-action reports. The system is included in the broader National Incident Management System (NIMS) established by FEMA as the standard for emergency management by all public agencies in the US. Increasingly, this approach is recommended to large private corporations to structure their responses, and many are doing so, albeit with mixed results.

In theory, and according to ICS doctrine, the system offers a uniform and transparent process for managing any imaginable incident. Due to the mandatory adoption of ICS across the US, there is a wide range of cases supporting its effectiveness in major, complex responses. For these reasons, many businesses see the value in at least understanding the system – if not fully implementing it themselves.

In this sense, ICS is the modern gold standard for centralized command and control of incident response (at least in the US). Interestingly, however, there is very little empirical evidence or academic research supporting its effectiveness. Indeed, quite a lot of debate surrounds the topic of its effectiveness.

It's a useful example of an off-the-shelf solution that can – in theory– be easily introduced into a complex corporate crisis response program. And it brings forward some very relevant and familiar principles, namely[2]:

- Modular organization: the notion that response organization can flex to meet the needs of the particular response;

- Management by Objectives: specific, measurable (aka "SMART") objectives drive incident operations from the top down;
- Every incident should have an incident action plan;
- Chain and Unity of Command; and Span of Control: everyone should have only one boss; the reporting lines are clear, and each boss should maintain a manageable ration of subordinates.
- Integrated Communications and comprehensive resource management.

All of this intuitively makes sense especially in a business context. However, many of the published, systematic reviews of ICS suggest there are problems when it is applied in complex settings. These problems may be familiar to experienced practitioners who often encounter the local version of ICS responses in various jurisdictions or settings. Even the simplified, condensed versions of ICS trainings run to 60 pages or more of material. It seems in practice that the application of ICS is often highly customized to meet individual needs, despite its seeming flexibility. This is especially true in the private sector context.

In the "Great ICS Debate" episode of their EPIC Podcast,[3] Dr. Joshua Bezanson and Grayson Crockett summarized these points very neatly by pointing out some of the logical flaws with ICS – the set of preconditions that do not necessarily exist in a real disaster:

- **The existence of pre-identified resources that can be easily typed/ categorized.**
  In ICS theory, resources are expected to be organized by category, kind, type, size, capability, and other characteristics. This is intended to make resource ordering and dispatch more straightforward for all the involved jurisdictions. Resource management is supposed to involve acquisition or procurement processes that are understood, and are based on agreements with relevant parties.

  In actuality, the things that are most needed in a response may not necessarily lend themselves to easy categorizations. For example, the organization may require specific IT tools or legal expertise – potentially from vendors with whom there was no preexisting agreement.
- **The use of strategies and tactics that have a known or predictable outcome and a relationship with cause and effect that is known.**

ICS offers an excellent approach to management by objectives, and the commonly used "Planning P," maps out the process neatly. This is especially true in the manner with which ICS delineates between the strategic and the operational.

However, one of the steps in the process that is often glossed over is the correlation or alignment of ICS Strategies to ICS Tactics. In some cases, this relationship is clear and can be taken for granted. But, in more highly complex contexts, the ability to know with confidence that specific actions will have known outcomes cannot be presumed. Sometimes alignment between strategy and tactics – or more precisely cause and effect – gets taken for granted or lost in the shuffle around the Planning P.

- **A Community of practitioners that speak and share a common language.**
  A key finding of the 9/11 Commission Report and a subsequent improvement to NIMS and ICS was the notion of a common language. It noted that responders should seek to avoid using language that cannot be understood across jurisdictions. The classic example of this jargon is the old police "10-codes."

  A common exercise to illustrate this point in introductory ICS courses involves an instructor asking the class to draw a picture of a "bus" on a sheet of paper and hold it up. Inevitably there will be drawings of a lot of classic school buses, but also a couple of ambulances. This is because, in some parts of the country, first responders refer to certain kinds of emergency medical vehicles as "buses." Similarly, with the word "tank" – you will find illustrations of a military tracked vehicle, a man-portable breathing apparatus, an airborne firefighting plane, or a freestanding water storage structure. The point is clear, and the same confusion occurs in private sector business contexts where teams speak their own language of acronyms and expressions that are not well understood outside the unit.

Effectively, the argument is that rigidly applying ICS can introduce or create more complexity than it resolves. Today's business problems are complex and unprecedented and do not lend themselves easily to SMART objectives. The tools and teams needed to solve these kinds of problems are less likely to speak in common terminology and may have only passing familiarity with one another – especially in a private sector context.

ICS is a very good example of centralized incident response methodology. It benefits from a federal mandate and broad base of highly trained adherents, at least in the US. It performs very well in conditions where it has worked before, and where the responders are familiar with the incident type at hand: wildfires, natural disasters, floods, etc. However, it has significant limits as a system for responding to novel threats involving high levels of uncertainty, exceptionally limited knowability, and the need for a diverse set of responders who may not have worked together before.

ICS does function well to establish a common understanding of what is real and what is not – something approaching joint sensemaking. But it does so often at a cost of time and manpower – and, again, most often in familiar types of responses. In other words, ICS is most effective at telling the kinds of "stories" it already knows. But it isn't as sharp a tool for defining an unfamiliar story in progress.

It may be the case that there are better ways of achieving these outcomes, particularly for today's large and complex enterprises.

The NASA funnel and go/no-go

One can hardly think of more complex, high-stakes activities than those associated with manned spaceflight. In this context, probably the best and most familiar example of effective creation of a common reality is the NASA Launch Status Check – or "go/no-go poll." This is familiar to many of us from TV and movies depicting Space Shuttle launches – the dramatic control room scenes depicting the NASA Test Director running down a checklist for final confirmation of all the key systems before launching the astronauts into space.

Indeed, NASA does deploy some of the finest formal problem-solving and emergency response techniques, bringing together diverse scientific and engineering disciplines to confront exceedingly challenging problems and glitches. One way they achieve this is to funnel problem-solving in a quasi-crowd sourcing approach where, for example, 300 experts on an issue might be brought to bear initially. Their responses to the problem will be whittled down to 100 experts, then 30, then a small core group for a final decision.

The approach illustrates the interplay between time, levels of involvement, and the ability to bring expertise to bear on a problem. The NASA-style method enables the organization to bring many more people to bear on a problem – even in limited time. This problem-solving style works very well for hard sciences and engineering problems.

But it doesn't, for obvious reasons, as easily lend itself to complex business problems. As problem-solving methods, both ICS and the NASA approaches are deductive. They depend on inferences about known quantities to make judgments or evaluate solutions to new problems. This works very well in conditions where the variables can be well understood – such as the hard sciences or routine, standardized first responder resources. However, while some problems in a business setting may be clearly defined, often that isn't the case. There may be significant disagreement over the nature of the problem, or the existence or relevance of various risks, and there may be no readily available means of measuring the potential outcome of courses of action.

How does a complex organization get high-quality people to weigh in without compromising the quality of decision-making?

The emergence of an international standard for crisis management

There is an effort underway to address some of the complexity around crisis management in the private sector, and the seeming need for a standard approach, which is taking place at the time of this writing with the ISO Technical Committee working on a new Standard. ISO 22361 is intended to serve as the international standard for good practice guidelines on crisis management.

The publication of this standard will be a significant advancement in the discussion around some of the questions posed here. Namely, according to the committee working on the standard, it will provide guidance for:

- "understanding the context and challenges of crisis management;
- developing an organization's crisis management capability through preparedness (see 5.5);
- recognizing the complexities facing a crisis team in action;
- communicating successfully during a crisis; and
- reviewing and learning."[4]

What is interesting about the approach being taken, however, is that it is

> ... specifically intended for management with strategic responsibilities for the delivery of a crisis management capability. It is for those who operate under the direction and within policy of **top management** in:
>
> - implementing the crisis plans and structures; and
> - maintaining and assuring the procedures associated with the capability.[5]

It is too soon to evaluate the Standard at this stage. The emphasis on "top management" is not unexpected or unreasonable. However, the hope will be that this standard can serve to build or advance crisis management capabilities broadly within an organization – and not only within its senior leadership. The ideal plan will not exclude those at the edges of the organization.

Some of the key features likely to follow from this Standard are:

- A role for governance (ideally, not just centrally but at all levels).
- Discussion around the creation of strategic capabilities for crisis management, which speaks to the value and importance of such a capability as well as its ability to set objectives and command resources.
- Focus on decision making and the need to clearly understand stakeholder interests.
- A foundation in ethical principles.
- Organizational learning as a foundational value of a good crisis management program.

There will be room for defining the effectiveness of crisis management programs. Some of the key features there will acknowledge the importance of early recognition of an incident or crisis; note the distinction between incidents and crises; facilitate a capability for quickly analyzing situations to establish strategies (what we'll refer to here as "sensemaking"); establish a common understanding of the principles underpinning a crisis response; and lead from a culture that supports these principles generally. The trick will be to ensure that these activities are not confined to the realm of the crisis team or the "top management" echelons alone.

With a good basis in an international standard as a point of reference, the questions then become when and how to implement such programs. In other words, what does good look like?

The challenge

What does good look like?

Living Companies, Arie de Geus and Separating the Winners and the Losers

What do these entities have in common?

* Sumitomo Group, a Japanese *keiretsu* diversified business enterprise with holdings ranging from automotive to insurance to materials and construction, and
* Stora Enso, a Swedish/Finnish manufacturer of pulp, paper, and forest products.

They are "living companies," according to Arie de Geus, author of the 1997 book by the same name.

At nearly 500 and 700 years of age, respectively, Sumitomo and Stora are among the oldest continuously operating companies in a world where the average life expectancy of a corporation is less than 20 years.

De Geus identified Sumitomo and Stora, along with about 30 other companies (including DuPont, W.R. Grace, Mitsui) that were over 100 years old, as part of a study he conducted during his tenure at Royal Dutch Shell as the head of their Strategic Planning Group.

But these two companies stand out as dramatic examples of resilience if one considers their age alone. Stora survived the European Middle Ages, the Reformation, the various wars of the 1600s and 1800s, the Industrial Revolution, and the two 20th-century World Wars, unaided by the incredible changes that came with the modern information age. Sumitomo was no different – and remarkably both companies remained continuously in business through all those centuries of change.

What stands out about these companies that enable this longevity? What do they have that the average 20-year-old business lacks when it meets its end? In other words – what separates the winners from the losers over the long term? According to de Geus it is the following:

> "Living companies" such as Sumitomo and Stora are good at managing change in a world that they admit they don't control.

This implies the acceptance of a certain level of powerlessness concerning the external environment. This admission is not something that comes easily to corporations or, certainly, to their leaders who may reflexively reject the appearance of uncertainty or weakness. But "living companies" share four characteristics – traits that also help explain their longevity.

The four shared personality traits of living companies[6]

1. Conservatism in Financing.
2. Sensitivity to the World around Them.
3. Awareness of Their Identity.
4. Tolerance of New Ideas.

These traits contribute to a corporate identity that evolves in harmony with the world around it – rather than in conflict with it, or at the whim of circumstances. The companies that embody these qualities have a clear sense of self: they know who they are, how they relate to the world around them, and they value their money in a way that provides flexibility for the future. Most important of all – they value new ideas and new people in a way that has enabled them to renew their businesses generation after generation.

It is precisely this fourth trait – the tolerance of new ideas – which is most important to long-term adaptability. The long-lived companies in de Geus' study tolerated activities on the margin. They allowed for experiments and eccentricities within their operations – within reason – that pushed understanding beyond optimizing core business alone. And, in keeping with the acceptance of the unknown, they also recognized that 1) some of these experiments could result in new businesses entirely unrelated to the core business; and 2) the act of starting a new business **need not be centrally controlled.**

De Geus offers the example of W.R. Grace – a company viewed today as an American specialty chemical and materials company. The company's history stretches back to the mid-1800s and reflects a long tradition of innovation leading to adaptation in a changing world. The company was founded in Peru in 1854 by Irish immigrant William Russel Grace, and initially focused on export of guano (i.e. bird droppings) from South America as a powerful fertilizer. Within a few years, the company had established its own merchant shipping line and moved its headquarters to New York City. Seeing the new opportunity presented by flourishing trade between the US, South America, and Europe, the company expanded further into transportation and by the 1920s partnered with Pan American World Airways to establish the first commercial aviation link between North and South America. In more recent decades, the enterprise expanded globally and into new markets and ventures, including banking, technologies, materials, consumer beverage, sports retail, etc. The W.R. Grace experience reflects the kind of innovation that enables an enterprise to transcend world events – World Wars, the Great Depression, entire Industrial Revolutions. It achieves success not by depending on the power and influence of individual leaders or single moments of inspiration. Rather, it compounds its progress year after year as a living company by being responsive to the world around it, and being reflective of its own identity without being dogmatic. This approach allows for exploration within its ranks into entirely new businesses that may fail, but may succeed and bring the company into new industries and eventually into new eras.

What do living companies tell us about how crisis teams can win?

According to de Geus, the key to longevity in business depends on a company having a basic personality reflective of the traits above, which are also driven by values that define the priorities for how managers lead, down to the front line.

Understandably, crisis managers don't necessarily have the influence over high-level company strategy that de Geus argues is needed for living companies. Indeed, it isn't a crisis team's mandate to build a company's legacy for decades to come. But, what crisis managers and crisis teams do have is influence at times that matter most – and sometimes the crisis defines the future for an enterprise. This can be for the better – or for the worst. How does the story of the crisis unfold – and how do the decisions that are made in the moments that matter most –impact the history and ultimate fate of an organization?

With this in mind, crisis teams can adopt a values-based mindset to their work that reflects the larger goals thinkers like de Geus had in mind. What are the priorities managers at living companies set for themselves and their workers?

- **Be Adaptive**. De Geus studied 27 long living companies. Every one of them changed their primary business portfolio at least once. DuPont, for example, in its nearly 200 years of operations, has pivoted from its origins as a gunpowder company to becoming a primary share-holder of General Motors (in the 1920s) to its current form as a specialty chemical company. The reason living companies can succeed in these transitions is that they value *people* not *assets*. Make no mistake, these organizations are not completely altruistic. They are motivated by profit and growth like any other business. But they can persist through time and violent change because they recognize that assets will come and go, but people are the life of their business – and that needs to remain their priority. Crisis teams can recognize this: change and adaptation can be supportive of – even driven by – the people in the organization.

- **Relax Steering and Control**. This may be the most relevant value for crisis teams and their clients (i.e. the decision makers they seek to influence). Living companies in de Geus' research gave their people the flexibility and tools to develop new ideas. More importantly, they provided freedom from control, direction, and the fear of failure around pursuing new innovation. This is a powerful way to put the value of adaptation and trust in people into action. During times of crisis response, bringing forward new ideas from the front lines of operations – quickly – can be critical. Reflecting back to von Moltke's ideas on leadership in war, this can support escalating options to local decision makers that might not have been immediately apparent at higher levels of the organization.

- **Adopt a Growth and Learning Mindset**. Living companies are organized for learning. Their experience shows what evolution looks like – and it isn't easy. Once a company has adapted to the new environment, it is no longer the organization it used to be. In the case of W.R. Grace, transitioning from exporting bird droppings from Peru to operating an international airline in the span of a few decades is astonishing to think about. Today we take rapid changes for granted to a certain extent, but this transition from the 1880s to the 1920s also spanned a World War and major developments in technology. Companies that endure these changes and succeed in these adaptations recognize change as the essence of learning. Teams of disparate people train intensively together and at regular intervals. This practice brings together the disparate disciplines, cultures, background, and professions within the enterprise in a way that supports growth and innovation. Crisis teams are no exception – bringing cross-functional teams together is their bread-and-butter. Building a training program around a learning mindset like this is critical.

- **Who are We?** De Geus' fourth priority for managers in living companies was to ensure that the company created a community. In other words, to ensure a long-lived organization that is profitable and adaptive to the world around it, it has to define its membership, establish common values, and live up to a human contract that exists in harmony with the world around it. This can be thought of along the lines of the contemporary language around diversity and inclusion. Companies need to be aware that they hold certain values in common with the communities in which they operate. They need to protect these values, and support employees in upholding them, in a way that leads to a shared identity and belief in a greater cause that everyone in the organization can connect with. Living companies seem more like "living work communities" than purely economic machines. However, in times of crisis, these values may be forcefully challenged. Some may seek to compromise them for the sake of short-term outcomes. The lesson from living companies is that this doesn't need to be the case.

The living companies offer a picture of what good can look like. Ultimately, these kinds of organizations stand a better chance of persevering in a world that they do not control. This is especially true when the notion of loosening control – and letting go of *centrally controlling* everything – factors in.

During a response, the crisis team still needs to understand how to orient itself quickly to the rapidly changing world around it. Instead of adapting to evolving conditions over decade-long time frames like a living company, the organization in crisis needs to identify itself in relation to the "crisis world" around it – and fast.

The solution

The company in crisis must bring the story to life – in the present

The living companies navigate the changing world around them through time and over epochs. Meanwhile, the companies that manage through acute crises do the aforementioned things well. They become unconquerable. In doing so, they prioritize and do the following effectively:

- Recognize triggering events quickly,
- Focus on initial objectives and practice iterative leadership,
- Always appropriately address stakeholders, and above all
- Accept the unknowability and uncertainty of their circumstances.

It seems clear that there can be quite a lot of overlap between these priorities and those of living companies. Especially in how the organization connects with its stakeholders; and the extent to which it reflects a willingness to admit to the ambiguity of its circumstances.

The idea that a crisis is an unfolding story, one that draws the organization and its crisis team in and demands participation, brings the conversation directly to leadership and decision-making. But before confronting that question, how do we proceed to "tell the story" of the unfolding crisis – especially in a highly integrated or complex organization?

Confronting uncertainty and knowability

In other words, how can the crisis team best aid in the service of good decision-making? This will depend on a great many factors – some of which will be exogenous or outside the control of the crisis team or the organization itself. Other factors, however, will be very much within the control of the relevant decision makers.

Under normal conditions, company leaders or executives might have a great deal of confidence in an organization's "readiness." However, in acute conditions – where the unexpected has occurred – the triggering event could impact leaders' ability to lead. This can occur either on an individual level or an organizational one. The overwhelming volume of incoming information, the sheer significance of the event itself, or a range of other factors could cause delays or errors in properly assessing the initial facts. This is not uncommon.

In these situations, the crisis management practitioners are often the ones who are expected to help leaders lead, to clear the distractions, and bring order to chaos.

In response to any triggering event – a natural disaster, terrorist attack, explosion, or even a product issue like a recall or a reputation matter – there will be an initial period of time where *Knowability* and *Uncertainty* present themselves as forces acting in opposite directions. This is commonly referred to as "the fog of war," and has inspired phrases like "the first report never looks like the last."

> As **knowability decreases**, responder's preconceived ideas for handling situations lose value. Organizations can tend to present their own obstacles to developing a common operating picture. And even documentation itself can become a hindrance rather than a benefit.
>
> On the other hand, as **uncertainty increases** pre-existing plans and blue-sky assessments become less useful. Rational analysis and clear thinking become increasingly difficult as uncertainty deepens. And the role of biases becomes a significant risk to good decision making.

The style and effectiveness of any crisis response will vary depending upon the influence of the forces of knowability and uncertainty on the responders and their decision makers. Some crises are completely unique, unprecedented events that leave no preconceived ideas for how to respond. Examples of these are the cascading events around the Fukushima disaster or the 9/11 attacks. Other crises present more like "incidents" which are variations on more familiar themes: hurricanes, winter storms, and floods. In cases such as these, there can be a basis for templates or patterns of response. It is important to note that even here significant deviations from the *expected* can occur.

As if this weren't difficult enough, add to these complications the intense focus in recent years on the controversy and political commentary that quickly surrounds so many incidents – often aided and amplified by social media. In settings like that the crisis management process itself can become deeply controversial.

There are, however, several managerial functions that can serve to enhance the effectiveness of crisis management efforts, form the basis of good decision making, and serve as a check to the objectivity of the responding teams. Early recognition of a triggering event, sensemaking and meaning-making are among these.

Early recognition of a triggering event

It is probably written in every book on crisis management that once a crisis manifests itself, the crisis team must take measures to deal with the consequences. This seems obvious. But as was clear in the case of the Alaska air traffic controllers, reality is much more complex. And in the real world, not all crises present themselves with a loud bang.

Effective management of a crisis depends upon a capability for shared recognition that a threat has emerged, or a risk has manifested itself, and that the circumstances demand immediate attention.

Whereas much traditional crisis management guidance will emphasize the role of extensive planning, playbooks, and forecasting in building this capability, that need not be the only approach. While there is a role for planning, it has its limits. To assist in filling that gap – and to improve the overall ability to develop this shared recognition early on – the organization beyond the crisis team (but perhaps led by it) can establish a practice of *foresight*. This will come into play later in the book as it relates to a role for intelligence and analysis in crisis management. But for the sake of early recognition and rapidly establishing a shared understanding, there are two conditions that matter most for establishing foresight:

- **Enable those on the periphery or the edges of the organization**. As Arjen Boin et al. observe (and quote Klein), there is extensive experience among system operators and first responders as to the dynamics of their operations during incidents. For example, firefighters often have a highly developed sense of impending danger. Operators of systems (even business or commercial systems) often have a highly attuned sense of their condition and an advanced ability recognize small deviations from the norm in complex but known processes. There are people with an innate ability to sense intuitively where things will go wrong and how things need to work.

    This kind of intuition is common among individuals other than first responder professions – for example, meteorologists, homicide detectives, and chefs. To put this another way, there is enormous value in building trust in the organization's intuition. And developing a capability to bring that valuable information forward in a structured way.

- Secondly, **do this by organizing support for those people** so that the enterprise has a process for rapid detection of impending threats. A premium can be placed on continuous vigilance and the willingness to act on even faint signals. The key is to develop an ability to build indicators for deviance in a process and a common pattern for escalation or action on those indicators.

These activities will understandably generate new streams of data and information that need processing, during times when the ability to process information is strained.

This leads to the concept of *sensemaking* and reinforces the idea that those on the periphery can be best suited to participate in the process of reaching agreement on a common picture of what is taking place. And that, once again, these activities do not only need to be centrally controlled.

Analysis paralysis

Very soon after a triggering event is recognized – call it an incident, a crisis, an emergency – there are demands for action and decisions to be made. As already discussed, the context in the early moments can be difficult to clarify or understand. Information may be incorrect, in short supply or overwhelming.

There are crisis management theorists who advise that a sequence of steps be followed in these conditions: first, collect and assess information, then define the current situation in writing, then propose a strategy, define tactics, assign resources, etc. In actuality, it may sometimes work this way – but more likely it does not. The implication is that decisions can – and should – be made following some assessment and that this assessment can be considered reliable and of service to good decision making.

This follows from the Western rational paradigm in which most businesses operate: information is good, more is better, and the better the analysis the better the decision. This is how we optimize systems under normal conditions, and it lends itself to scientific inquiry or linear processes.

There are other crisis management thinkers who point out that the decision-making and assessment processes do not need to be sequential in this way. Rather, they should be inverted – such that the quickly needed decision even precedes the analysis of the situation. Or that both the analysis and the decision-making are intertwined and iterative.

Sometimes – especially in confrontation with the unexpected – decisions need to be made in the absence of information. Conditions may not allow for complete analysis, but a decision is still needed.

What do we do in that case?

Sensemaking – what's the story?

Sensemaking is a concept that has its origins in social psychology, first used by organizational theorist Karl Weick in 1969. The term literally refers to the act of "making sense." It refers to a process of identifying order where none may exist or the ability to make sense of an ambiguous situation.

In the context of crisis management a quote from Weick stands out:

> Sensemaking involves "being thrown into an ongoing, unknowable, unpredictable streaming of experience in search of answers to the question, **'What's the story?'**"[7]

Another way of putting this is to think of sensemaking as a process of creating situational awareness in settings with rapidly eroding *knowability* and rapidly increasing *uncertainty*.

> Imagine, for example, a person being asked to play a game, without knowing the rules or possessing a rulebook. As each player makes a move, the new player will attempt to understand their motives and objectives. Through trial and error, the player makes moves and responds to signs of acceptance or disapproval from members of the group. Eventually the rules are understood in a way that enables strategic decision making in the game. In a sense, this is like creating a map of what cannot be seen – feeling forward through the fog.

This is critical in crisis response – especially in the earliest stages. If the response stands still to clarify data in the fog, they stay in the fog. But by taking *action* they create new information in the form of feedback – both positive and negative. In some cases, this means that the team has to act in order to make progress. This is how the map gets written on the fly in the presence of ambiguity – and this is how better decisions can be created where no good options seem to exist.

The process can be structured, but it doesn't have to be.

To enable sensemaking – at least within the crisis team and the leadership group – a few steps can be taken:

- **Scan the immediate landscape**
  Quickly evaluate the current information landscape to broadly identify several key factors, some of which should already be known prior to the triggering event.
  - Identify immediately critical stakeholders.
  - Triage information. "Bucket" or categorize the types of incoming information flow and characterize but don't analyze. (Too much of this, too little of that).
    - Clarify "interpretations," "emotions," "problem situations," and "prior knowledge."
- **Seek out divergent opinions**
  Rapid consensus is not necessarily the goal. Inviting opinions that differ from the initial judgments about the circumstances is crucial to quickly reach a well-balanced map of the circumstances. This is also

the check against biases that will influence thinking under stressful conditions. The simplest way to obtain a different perspective is to ask the question, "What are we missing here?"

- **Iterate by testing assumptions continuously**

  Accept that decision-making under these conditions is different from decision-making the organization or business might be used to. In sensemaking, the actions and decisions interact with each other quickly and progress needs to be constantly evaluated.

  This is a learn-by-doing approach and so the team may make progress down one path only to discover the need to redirect or backtrack based on new information. That is not a detriment or a failure of this process – rather, it is indicative of progress and is expected.

  The purpose of the exercise is to continuously "map" or represent the problem situation, challenge it with new data, and discard or modify the new representation of the problem situation.

- **Adopt multiple perspectives**

  The leadership team may have a perspective that is focused on one risk, while the operations team may see percolating problems in another area.

  In some cases, a normally peripheral function may have to be placed front-and-center for a period of time to place emphasis where it is needed. In complex situations, having the ability to rapidly bring subject matter experts to bear on the sensemaking and decision iteration should be a core competency of the crisis management team.

- **Drive iteration and action**

  The sensemaking process extends beyond initial data gathering and decision iteration. The process of collecting feedback and redefining the map will continue while decisions and actions return new clarifications. Eventually, the response will adopt a stable or balanced momentum and the crisis team can guide this process with less immediate urgency. But in the early stages, it is critical to keep the wheel moving and not fall back into analysis paralysis.

The crisis team are the mapmakers

While this process unfolds, the map of the situation will come together like a maze – including the paths that lead nowhere, the paths that remain unclear and those that may lead to an exit.

The crisis team should lead the building and maintenance of the map – and help brief new stakeholders who come to the table to comprehend it. The easiest way to keep this current is to focus on the narrative that unfolds – what is the story the situation is telling, how is the team influencing the story, and what will the next chapter say?

To answer this as the situation evolves, the crisis team has to manage the competing dynamics of time pressure, the level of involvement of appropriate stakeholders, and the ability to bring the most relevant expertise to bear. By becoming the mapmakers, the crisis team is in a position to best manage these dynamics against knowability and uncertainty in the service of good decision-making.

The leadership challenge – make everyone the problem owner

The interplay between the decision-making and sensemaking processes can also be structured. While there are some who argue that the sensemaking process must *always* precede decision-making, this is not absolute. It is for this reason that the process calls for bringing together multiple perspectives.

There is incredible value in bringing the players from the periphery or the edges of the organization into the sensemaking process.

But there can also be a phenomenon where those who are closest to operations – by virtue of their perspective – cannot understand the significance of what they see without leadership context. At the same time, leadership cannot take effective action if it misses the valuable, sometimes intuitive, understanding from the operations level. Either party can be standing so close to the problem that they "can't see the elephant" so to speak.

The solution is to turn the traditional process on its head.[8] Leadership – with support from the crisis team – must take a strong position. This book will talk more about the role of the crisis team later, but in summary for now the process can instead look like this, quite simply.

- The decision makers telegraph to the team that they will make a decision. That the decision will be made with or without them.
- The decision makers request information from the operations teams related to the decision. This is stated as a request for information that they *know to be relevant*. The leaders emphasize that they want to depend on the operations teams' intuition.

- The operations teams direct their own information gathering processes strictly toward enabling that decision. They ignore unrelated information.

Ultimately, decisions are decisions. They are always the same – and they only come in a few varieties (communications, loss of services, etc). Through a process of soliciting feedback from their operations, leaders can learn (and be coached) to drive toward common decision themes. The question is simply, what information is needed to make the decision – not what decision does the totality of available information suggest.

"Treat the problem as an experiment"[9]

Making everyone a problem owner helps position the organization to start joint sensemaking. This brings the decision-making process closer to the incoming information and helps keep biases and analysis paralysis at bay.

The bottom line is that in moments of crisis, treating the problem as an experiment frees the organization to act against spiraling uncertainty. This is just the sort of thing that living companies do as part of their everyday business – tolerating new ideas, maintaining awareness of stakeholders, and pulling in good ideas from front-line intuition. At the same time, it should be clear that in the crisis context this is not innovation. There should be no illusion that when the unexpected happens a "plant a thousand flowers" approach will work.

On the contrary – organizations confronted with crisis need to be willing and able to buck their normal systems to allow agility to win the day. There are a lot of ideas about how crisis teams can support this, but the evidence seems to show that those who can map the unfolding situation quickly, make sense of the story that is coming together, and learn quickly to play by the new rules will endure better than those who focus only on planning and playbooks and hierarchies.

TAKEAWAY

- There are traditional and orthodox approaches to crisis management that have value in responding to familiar or more commonly occurring incidents. In such scenarios – like natural disasters or routine emergencies – these approaches can work well for managing and assigning resources. However, these approaches are also limited when responding to novel crises – and can even fall flat when the routine emergencies present unexpected outcomes. The increasing frequency and severity of today's incidents, as well as the fact that novel disasters seem to be occurring more regularly, call for a more adaptive approach.

- The challenge is that there are companies in existence today that have overcome centuries of upheaval and navigated the same complexity of changes and crises we often think of as unique to modern times. In doing so, these so-called living companies offer lessons for today's crisis teams at any organization. Namely: they are adaptive to circumstances; willing to pivot into uncharted areas; willing to loosen centralized control; and define for themselves a clear identity.
- Today's crisis teams must bring the story of a crisis situation to life in the present, build an unfolding map of the circumstances it is presenting and guide iterative decision making from the beginning.
- To achieve this, those in operations at the edges of the organization must be linked to the crisis management team and welcomed into joint sensemaking.
- At times, bold decision making will be required in the absence of a clear direction. But this is often exactly what is needed in order to clarify the next steps.

Notes

1. https://training.fema.gov/emiweb/is/icsresource/assets/glossary%20 of%20related%20terms.pdf, p. 6.
2. https://training.fema.gov/emiweb/is/icsresource/assets/ics%20review% 20document.pdf
3. *EPIC Podcast* – Dr.Joshua Bezanson and Grayson Cockett, Episode: 10/09/2021 – "The Great ICS Debate."
4. https://www.isotc292online.org/projects/iso-22361/
5. Ibid.
6. Arie de Geus. "The Living Company," *Harvard Business Review Magazine* March–April 1997, https://hbr.org/1997/03/the-living-company%C2%A0%20-
7. K. E. Weick, K. M. Sutcliffe, and D. Obstfeld, "Organizing and the process of sensemaking," Organizational Science, Vol. 16, No. 4, 2005, pp. 409–421.
8. Interview, Arjen Boin, 10/14/2021.
9. Ibid.

PART II

4

CRISIS MANAGEMENT FOR COMPLEX ORGANIZATIONS

A practical approach

How can complex organizations *program* for readiness when the unexpected happens? Understanding the limits of planning, what should organizations do to be "ready?"

What if crisis management didn't have to be only a highly centralized activity? If the companies that emerge from crisis better than they went in succeed by connecting to the edges of the organization, what is the role of the crisis team?

How can leaders be positioned to make bold but effective decisions?

What are the guiding principles of a crisis management function within a complex organization?

The answers to these questions have to do with the ability to grow "crisis competencies" throughout an organization: in leadership, among the crisis team, but also at the edges. In so doing, the organization becomes better positioned to quickly identify when a potential crisis is brewing and act accordingly. This may sound like a tall order. But if we focus on Planning

DOI: 10.4324/9781003216803-6

for Effects rather than Causes, it turns out there are really only three possible *effects* of all crises: unexpected loss of people, places, or things.

In response to these crises, experience also shows that there are generally only a few "flavors" or types of crisis that are likely to occur.

With these concepts in mind, there may be a practical approach to building a culture of readiness – and consequently improved crisis management – even at the most complex organizations.

Quite simply, it comes down to the ability to ask and answer three questions: Who's in Charge, What Needs to Be Done, and Who's Doing What? This book will explore each of these in more detail. But first it seems sensible to present the basic concept of programming for readiness in the most practical terms and build from there.

"Blue sky days"

This book will explore the only three questions you need to ask (Who's in Charge, What needs to be Done, and Who's Doing What?) in detail in subsequent chapters. The approach to these questions can help define an organizational response to the unexpected that results in far better outcomes and lives up to the values a company sets out for itself – hopefully aligned with those of living companies, for example. This forms the basis of a crisis response that can make an organization unconquerable.

Much of that comes into play once the unexpected has materialized. Most of the time, however, organizations are not in crisis. These periods of relative peace or calm should reflect normal business operations when the usual challenges arise and are resolved by good, existing business practices. These can be referred to as "blue sky days."

Blue sky days are the perfect opportunity for an organization to contemplate how it might respond to unforeseen risks – and for those organizations with crisis management teams to engage in commonly recognized planning and training activities. An organization may adopt a very traditional approach, sticking to ICS methods and adhering to playbooks and planning materials. On the other hand, it may take a radically different approach and fully trust in its ability to respond to anything adaptively.

Guiding principles of a crisis management function

Whichever approach it follows, a concrete set of guiding principles should be considered as core to the crisis management function. Regardless of the planning appetite, incorporating guiding principles will lead to leaner, more responsive sensemaking and decision making, better initial recognition of triggering events, and more effective early response. Guiding principles are foundational.

Each of these principles corresponds with one of the Big Three Questions (Who's in Charge, What needs to be Done, and Who's Doing What?).

1. **Establish a crisis management governance framework**

    A crisis management function is dependent upon well-understood roles, responsibilities, and competencies. This should be true of any function in any well-run business. But in the case of crisis management, the ability of employees at any level to respond capably is directly related to their understanding of these factors. To be effective, the governance principle can only be adopted during blue sky days – not while a crisis is in progress.

    Examples of activities under this principle may include the following:

    o Establish and manage a governance infrastructure. This should include the creation of, or enhancement to, a high-level but uniform crisis management policy and a common language around crisis management in the organization.

    o Set expectations for a consistent and transparent approach, to planning activities, the need for these planning activities, and the adoption of any related crisis management systems or tools. Emphasize the high-level goals of a streamlined response in the event of a disruption.

    o Identify and use existing functional processes and personnel to monitor and report on capabilities – as well as potential opportunities.

    o Ensure senior leaders are aware of, and familiar with, the crisis management function's ability to provide decision-making support.

2. **Launch crisis management as a strategic capability**

    To effectively bring in actionable information and intelligence from the operational front line in support of response activities, crisis management needs to be clearly regarded as a strategically important function. While it is likely, with luck, that most people in an organization will not directly hear from their crisis management team, it is important for them to know that one is there, it has the full faith of the organization, and all members of the organization have a role to play when the time comes.

Examples of activities supporting this principle may include the following:

o   Incorporate the crisis management capability into the organization's core values statements, mission documents, or priorities.
o   Ensure that the crisis management function is aligned with these core values.
o   Integrate the crisis management function into Strategic and Operational Functions to the extent practical.
o   Consider appointing a senior staff leadership and governance committee for crisis management.
o   Reinforce and clarify the value placed on early reporting of operational deviations.
o   Integrate crisis management into enterprise risk management processes as a partner. They will also be able to assist with understanding the impact on the company's risk assessment should a critical risk manifest itself unexpectedly.

3. **Support readiness through learning: coaching and exercising**

    One of the most value-added blue sky day activities for a crisis management team involves exercises. The book will explore this in great detail later, but it may be worth considering these activities as a principle in and of themselves.

    As we have shown, planning does not necessarily equal readiness. And readiness itself can be an elusive goal. The crisis competencies that an organization needs to navigate through a situation are perishable. For these reasons, building a function that values *learning* through coaching and exercises is of great value.

    Examples of activities under this principle may include the following:

    o   Empower the crisis team to partner across functional, market, project, business, and international lines. Enable the crisis team to coordinate with internal subject matter experts, operations teams, and external partners.
    o   Facilitate regular scenario-based exercises (tabletop or otherwise) not primarily for the purpose of assessing effectiveness, but rather for the purpose of challenging the crisis management governance and associated protocols. Use exercises to test the protocols for improvement.

- Consider internal and external benchmarking to identify trends and scan the horizon for best practices.
- Establish the crisis management function as a meaningful advisor to the business, both in response and on blue sky days.

4. **Build trust in the organization, build trust with the community**

   A major element of the successful crisis management function that is often overlooked is the time and energy needed to develop and maintain meaningful relationships. To guide an enterprise through crisis optimally, the crisis team must have the trust of the organization when it matters most. This trust cannot be earned "on the battlefield;" instead it has to emerge from positive relationships, ideally formed over time.

   More broadly, the crisis team – and hopefully the organization as a whole – recognizes the value of building trust with the community of which they are a part. Living companies are expert in building trust. Bringing together a clear corporate identity rooted in values, upholding the highest ethical standards, and acting as responsible corporate citizens in all aspects of stakeholder engagement is critical. The crisis team specifically will be called upon to help leaders lead at times when individual and collective pressure or temptation to compromise ethics may be at their greatest. The team must be prepared to navigate these pressures and ensure decision-making, ethics, and communication can remain focused and objective.

   Examples of putting this principle into action may include:

   - Ensure the organization can communicate accurate, credible, and timely reports to stakeholders, consider a blue sky activity to generate pre-approved communications and media holding statements or templates to streamline the review and drafting process during response.
   - Ensure that the ethics and values are represented in balance with brand and reputation. If the organization has an ethics/compliance function, it should be represented on the broader crisis management team as a stakeholder and subject matter expert.
   - In exercises and responses, bring in ethical and values-based discussion. Consider asking questions that get to the heart of honesty/integrity, boldness, curiosity, and accountability such as:
     - Are we acting with clear intent?
     - Are we actively listening to ideas and concerns? Are these perspectives valued?
     - Have we questioned the impact of our decisions?

- Are we prepared to demonstrate the responsibility we have for our decisions (when these decisions may prove to be wrong, or iterative)?
  - Establish a monitoring and reporting capability within the crisis team to coordinate assessments on readiness and provide reports to leadership as a form of accountability.
  - Engage with internal and external partners to build relationships on a blue sky basis to gain perspective on readiness levels, activities, and tools. Partners can include internal functions, markets, geographies as well as peer companies, competitors (appropriately), advisory firms, government agencies, response organizations, and professional associations.

These principles are foundational guideposts for establishing the kind of crisis management program that makes an organization *unconquerable*. These are the building blocks necessary to serve the needs of the business and its leaders while honoring – or even building – the faith and respect of stakeholders across the organization and externally. The specific guiding principles at an organization will vary depending on its specific mission, values, composition, and goals. But they should reflect a balance of governance, strategic partnership, a learning orientation, and a basis in ethics around building trust. Note, some of these guiding principles reflect concrete actionable or structural recommendations. Others, however, are clearly cultural. And they all should be informed by the broader community and cultural context of the organization. "Culture is King," as the saying goes. Obviously, corporate culture has become recognized as a competitive advantage in modern times. But nothing will lay plain the truth of a company's culture like a genuine crisis. If the foundation is weak, the structure will fail. For the crisis team to have a role in making the company *unconquerable*, there needs to be some thought given to how a readiness culture can map to the broader company and community goals.

The readiness is all

In the Introduction and opening chapter, this book reflects on the nature of crisis, what it means to be *unconquerable*, and the increasing inevitability of the unexpected. We pondered the meanings of the words *crisis* and *disaster* themselves and how they relate to our ability to connect to the events unfolding before us.

There is a scene at the end of Hamlet where the prince finally stops his ceaseless, exhausting worrying and analyzing, and accepts that – come what may – all he can do is be ready. Hamlet admits that even the most insignificant thing ("...There is a special providence in the fall of a sparrow...") is guided by something greater than him. His only remaining responsibility, the only choice he has left, is to be poised to respond to whatever circumstances will throw at him next. As Hamlet tells his friend, Horatio, "...the readiness is all."

In large, complex organizations there is a lot of bandwidth and resources available for analysis, preparation, planning, and mitigation of every imaginable risk. Quite appropriately, a significant amount of energy should be invested on blue sky days in cataloguing the risks confronting an enterprise so that they can be managed. Organizations have a duty to provide this type of assurance to their stakeholders, in many cases they are required to do so, and it should be done in alignment with the company's values.

At times, however, these analyses and their associated work streams can take on a life of their own. This may create conditions where the confidence in the work product generated – the plans, the reports, etc. – can take the place of confidence in the ability to respond and recover. In other words, confidence in the planning process may supersede awareness of what the reality would look like of a risk truly manifesting itself, unexpectedly.

There is a semantic minefield in defining this concept with strong preferences for different language to express what may often be the same intent. There are those that favor the term "preparedness," others prefer variations of the theme of "resilience" (such as organizational resilience), and still others prefer terms like "recoverability." Some of these terms carry connotations from other fields of study like psychology or from practices like business continuity and disaster recovery.

Ultimately, the word choice may be simply a matter of taste. For the crisis management practitioner, what matters is that the crisis team can get the organization on board with the notions that

- unexpected things can happen;
- even if they seem familiar (like a common storm or outage) they can present with completely novel complications; and

- planning/analysis alone will not suffice. The organization needs to meet these circumstances head on.

This requires *readiness*.

On building a culture of readiness

Organizational leadership should foster a positive attitude across the board among employees and stakeholders around the company's values, but the crisis management team should lead the creation of messaging around what it truly means to be *ready*. Acknowledging the semantics above, this can be done in a way that does not censure any preferences for other language (like resilience).

In fact, readiness should be regarded as a holistic element of the culture, which in addition to protecting the organization and its people, values, and business, can also serve to meet the needs of the business as they evolve. Above all, the concept of a culture of readiness has to emphasize *progress, not perfection*.

As such, a culture of readiness can recognize each of the following:

- **Risk management and awareness:** The formal practice of continually identifying and reviewing risks to the enterprise; assigning accountability for managing these; and guiding strategy based on findings from these assessments.
- **Commitment to crisis management:** Recognition of the capability in the organization to bring forward and mobilize key expertise in confrontation with unstructured, escalating, and unexpected events.
- **Forecasting and early warning:** Encouraging and rewarding the practice of identifying and appropriately escalating potential deviations – as a matter of blue sky operations, and during response. The leadership respects the challenge this poses to frontline workers and managers; and the frontline workers and managers understand their duty to act responsibly on their intuition.
- **Planning as a learning function:** The traditional planning processes may provide a level of comfort or consistency to the organization that is valuable. To that extent they should remain, and should emphasize the coaching and learning values that planning can offer. After action reports, exercises and plan reviews should not be considered

compliance or check-the-box activities, but real opportunities for both immediate learning and longer-term growth.

- **Communications and awareness:** Regular and transparent communications are enormously valuable to ensure that expectations are understood across the enterprise. Messaging should be rooted in the contemporary here-and-now by making reference to current real world examples of why the crisis management service is relevant. At the same time, the messaging should remain positive and upbeat – limiting the reliance on fear, uncertainty and doubt as a motivation. Readiness is not about "handling the bad stuff." It is about demonstrating that the unconquerable organization can take a hit and get back up – arguably stronger.

- **Psychological safety and the no fault baseline:** This is perhaps the most important aspect of building a culture of readiness. Firstly, the subject matter that crisis management practitioners deal with regularly can be off-putting or upsetting to uninitiated audiences. The team should recognize that. Second, to successfully integrate the edges into the center; to effectively *unboss* the response; to ensure the flow of information needed when it matters most; people across the organization must feel comfortable about the why's and how's of the crisis response. This goes to Planning as Learning, Forecasting/Early Warning, and Communications and Awareness. A no-fault baseline should be considered when implementing crisis response activities – especially those proposed here – so that stakeholders learn to trust that their input will be valued, their missteps in responses will not be admonished, blame is not assigned, decision making is necessarily iterative, and the ultimate goal will be *progress not perfection.*

For the unconquerable organization, the blue-sky day objective should be readiness on a collective level. Having teams of empowered staff and leaders who value agility and are willing to be adaptive, rather than dogmatic, takes skill and commitment.

Reaching this goal takes individual effort, especially on the part of leadership and the crisis team. But it is not their responsibility alone. Their task is also to create the conditions for growth of crisis competencies among all members of the organization. Among other things, this is what it takes to *unboss* the response capability.

Crisis competencies

A significant amount of research has been conducted into what qualities matter most for an organization to be "crisis ready." This research looks at the individual leadership characteristics, structural organizational variables, as well as management and external factors. The findings show that while tangible and structural qualities matter a great deal, there are also highly significant subjective features – individual characteristics even – that are common to high-performing organizations in crisis.

Predicting Organizational Crisis Readiness: Perspectives and Practices Toward a Pathway to Preparedness, from The Center for Catastrophe Preparedness and Response at NYU by Dr. Paul C. Light outlines organizational characteristics that enhance an organization's ability to recover after a crisis, drawing from a survey of opinion leaders from government, private sector, and nonprofit sectors to compare crisis characteristics of organizations. In doing so, Light sought to capture the essence of the term "crisis readiness."

Light's research identifies some of the characteristics of crisis readiness commonly observed among individuals and organizations:

Frequently mentioned external/environmental characteristics[1]

- o Monitoring trends in the external environment.
- o Engaging in scenario planning.
- o Developing an early warning system and engaging in risk assessment.
- o Actively managing relationships with important stakeholders inside and outside of the organization (stakeholder management).

Frequently mentioned structural characteristics[2]

- o Building strong teams within the organization and managing them well.
- o Sharing authority throughout the organization by empowering subordinates while still maintaining a strong chain of command.
- o Creating flexible and efficient decision-making processes.
- o Designating responsibility for crisis readiness to one individual or a specific team.
- o Organizing fast, accurate, and efficient communication flows.

- ○ Adopting an organizational culture that values crisis management, safety, and resiliency.
- ○ Engaging in continuous improvement and learning. Encouraging creative solution development.
- ○ Building in structural redundancy.

Frequently mentioned leadership characteristics[3]

- ○ Generating buy-in and commitment.
- ○ Getting adequate resources for crisis readiness Institutionalizing concerns of the community and other stakeholders.
- ○ Recruiting and motivating a high-caliber workforce. Implementing sound day-to-day business management practices.
- ○ Taking a comprehensive approach to crisis readiness, and bridging gaps within the organization and between the organization's members and stakeholders.
- ○ Visioning a "a new business paradigm."
- ○ Developing trust within the organization.
- ○ Conducting vulnerability assessments.
- ○ Not letting risk aversion drive all decisions.
- ○ Actively engaging in learning.
- ○ Being aware of the special role of the leader.

Frequently mentioned management characteristics[4]

- ○ Developing and implementing crisis management/disaster management plans.
- ○ Incorporating crisis readiness into the strategic management process, the strategic plan, and the overall business planning process.
- ○ Engaging in a crisis management planning process and regularly updating the plan.
- ○ Engaging in risk and vulnerability assessment. Increasing staff crisis readiness through regular crisis drills.
- ○ Ensuring that the organization has sufficient general workforce training programs in place.
- ○ Rewarding error detection and reporting. Implementing robust project management systems.
- ○ Providing redundant, off-site locations to ensure continuity of operations.

Admittedly, much of the emphasis on these characteristics lies in what might be considered the preparation, planning, or mitigation phases of crisis management. Building upon Light's research, Montgomery Van Wart and Naim Kapucu's work in their article, "Crisis Management Competencies: The case of emergency managers in the USA"[5] seeks to clarify what competencies are needed in the response phase of crises.

Van Wart and Kapucu identified a profile of leadership in their data, which focused on emergency managers confronted with catastrophic disasters. Their findings showed three characteristics of effective crisis leaders and corresponding "clusters of competencies."

Briefly, these three primary leadership characteristics are:

1. Calmness in the face of adversity.
2. The ability to make pragmatic decisions under severe time/resource constraints.
3. An ability to balance "strength" with "routine" managerial coordination and organization.

For each of the characteristics, Van Wart and Kapucu mapped a set of perceived competencies.[6]

As an example, they point out that the need for calm, strong leadership would call for competencies such as the ability to project self-confidence, readiness to assume responsibility, the ability to express vision and mission, as well as resilience and communication skills.

In relation to pragmatism in decision making, competencies such as flexibility, decisiveness and the ability to delegate are highlighted. Lastly, soft skills such as networking, partnering and exercising social influence support the coordinate and organization characteristics.

Given the foregoing, two takeaways stand out which Paul Light observed: "Readiness appears to reside in a relatively small number of variables that organizations can control," and "Crisis management must be a lasting organizational commitment."[7]

While a menu of available options for competencies is quite informative, what is the best way to focus on those which the organization can best or most likely control? David Lindstedt very helpfully boils down many of Light's points into a set of "significant predictors of (organizational) crisis readiness"[8]:

The Organization:

- Engages in preparedness planning, training, and exercises.
- Has clear chains of command with leaders who share a vision of mission and encourage teamwork.
- Has high-performing, competent, competitive, results driven, and innovative employees.
- Is vulnerable to, threatened by, or has experienced external crisis.
- Regularly surveys clients and customers and actively monitors threats.
- Spends time and money on continuous improvement of crisis readiness.

Lindstedt and Armour later refined these further into a short list of crisis competencies[9]:

- Crisis Fortitude
- Leadership
- Performance
- Shared Vision
- Teamwork

These competencies can be considered the *manner in which* individuals and organizations achieve the "what" and "how" of crisis management related activities. Placing emphasis on developing these competencies across the organization – in a way that is meaningful to the people in the organization, consistent with its values and supportive of a culture of readiness– puts the business in a position of strength regardless of what may happen. In this way, an organization can program for readiness in a way that sees the value of planning, without having to be solely dependent upon the written plans themselves.

Toward a practical approach
The myth of the corporate crisis "first responder"

There is a persistent myth in the worlds of private sector crisis and security management that crisis or security teams can immediately swoop in to save the day in response to any potential threat impacting their organization.

Undoubtedly, in certain contexts there is cause for private sector security programs that are programmed this way. But even in these cases – usually in highly regulated industries – those responders are authorized by local jurisdictions and will ultimately always have to defer to public sector law enforcement and first responders.

But setting those situations aside, the myth remains around crisis management programs especially. In some cases, the myth is perpetuated by the company and its associates who are likely unfamiliar with legitimate crisis management capabilities and roles – and may have never had contact with their crisis management team. For this reason, there can exist a mystique around the small, mysterious team. This mystique can lead to a misguided, and potentially dangerous, expectation that the team capabilities are more in line with Hollywood movies than reality.

Worse yet, there are practitioners who fall into the trap of believing this myth themselves. This could be in part because the discipline attracts talent from the law enforcement, first responder and intelligence communities where a degree of compartmentalization, strict hierarchy, and classification of information is commonplace. The tendency can sometimes be to carry over habits of treating work product and activity as more clandestine than it needs to be. The other cause could be that the organization itself attributes importance to opacity because they don't understand the function, and it is simply easier or even beneficial for practitioners to perpetuate it.

Regardless of the reason, the notion of the "corporate smokejumper" or "first responder" is counter to many of the characteristics of successful crisis management programs. Rather than secret agents launched into unfamiliar territory, crisis management teams should be trusted advisors – transparent, recognized, and guided by the same set of common values as the rest of the organization's operations. Their role is not to swoop in and take command from the impacted operations or leaders, but to partner side by side with those people. By acting as guardians of a process that can offer solutions, they can truly be of *service* to decision makers and associates in need.

Complex organizations can *program* for readiness when the unexpected happens, in part by understanding the limits of planning, in part by building and maintaining strong relationships across the enterprise, and always by embodying community values. In this way, crisis management doesn't have to be only a highly centralized activity – and it certainly doesn't need to be hidden behind closed doors.

Rather, the companies that emerge from crisis better than they went in succeed by connecting to the edges of the organization, by extending the crisis team deep into all corners of the organization.

Think back to the *unboss* themes presented in the Introduction:

- **Everyone instead of the few.** The crisis team should take the shape of its container – not be confined to a small, predetermined team. Build a brand around your crisis response that includes the "many."
- **Mechanism vs structure.** Anything with moving parts is a mechanism; things that can only move as a whole are structures. When crisis strikes, the team should guide the response but not direct every aspect of it. Where needed and appropriate, parts and pieces should be able to move independently of the whole while keeping the entire organization moving toward the common goal.
- **Purpose instead of profit.** Being purposeful always matters, but never more so than when things are at their seeming worst. Acting with integrity and being transparent may not always improve the bottom line. But in today's world, it bears repeating that businesses can't survive in societies that fail.

Companies that *do well by doing good*, the living companies, embody these ideas. And bringing them into the crisis management at a program level – throwing open the doors of the program to the organization is a critical step. How can this be done as a practical matter?

Crisis management envoys and a crisis envoy network

The crisis management team can't do it all alone. Nor should they. As already discussed, the most valuable information needed for decision-making can very well reside on the front lines. The success of a response depends in large part upon early recognition of deviations – even subtle ones.

Crisis Management Envoys are respected and influential leaders and individual contributors within their areas of responsibility. They do not have to hold any specific job title, have any extensive background in crisis or emergency management (although it helps), or even be part of the official management structure. The requirements for a Crisis Management Envoy are the ability to act as a primary conduit between the core crisis management team and their business unit, to translate context and information between the center and the edges effectively, and to carry the vision and values of the crisis management to their business unit in a way that can be understood locally.

Crisis Management Envoys should be part of a broader network of Envoys representing every "jurisdiction" within the enterprise. In other words, every significant business unit should have a Crisis Management Envoy representing its interests and stakeholders, and these Envoys should establish contact with one another, with coordination by the core crisis management team. This will look different in every organization. Some organizational lines may be defined by geography, others by lines of business. In complex organizations, all of the above may be applicable. What matters is that the key stakeholders are identified and represented in a federation of sorts bringing together immediate access to all corners of the organization.

The qualities of Crisis Management Envoys should be supportive of the crisis competencies:

- Crisis Fortitude
- Leadership
- Performance
- Shared Vision
- Teamwork

They should be able to role model these competencies in a way that their specific organizational unit can connect with.

Some key responsibilities of a Crisis Management Envoy are:

- Serve as a primary point of contact between impacted stakeholders in their area and the core crisis team throughout real-world responses.
- Influence and lead local crisis planning activities, in coordination with the central team.
- Advocate openness and willingness to explore process improvements.
- Lead with a positive attitude relating to crisis response.

- Facilitate clear, concise and direct communication – dispel the myths and mystique surrounding crisis teams if they exist.
- Assist with issue identification and resolution.
- Provide input on crisis management communications.
- Receive and process feedback resulting from key messages.
- Facilitate regular meetings with local operations representatives.

The role of the core crisis management team is to create the impetus for the Crisis Management Envoy Network (Figure 4.1) – and to lead its coordination. The core team does not necessarily always need to lead the Network. In fact, it can be beneficial for the Envoys themselves to take greater ownership by adopting a rotating leadership or shared leadership of the Network. Nevertheless, the core crisis team should guide the agenda setting, lead by example in guiding discussions, and keep the team focused in the proper direction.

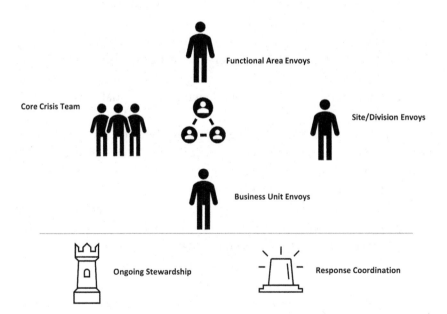

Crisis Management Envoys Network

Functional Area Envoys

Core Crisis Team

Site/Division Envoys

Business Unit Envoys

Ongoing Stewardship

Response Coordination

Figure 4.1 Ongoing collaboration across organizational lines among business units and the core crisis team.

The Network has two primary functions: *Stewardship* and *Response Coordination.*

During blue sky days, the Network will act as good stewards of their operations to the core crisis team. This means, among other things, each Envoy will ensure that proper, responsible planning and management of resources is underway to meet the desired level of readiness in their area. They will coordinate with the core team on needs or gaps they've identified locally (typically, training and exercise needs, or guidance on planning activities and local compliance).

As a practical matter, bringing the Network together on a stewardship basis should be done with some degree of regularity, depending upon the organization and its business. Annually might not be often enough, while monthly may be too much. A sweet spot for many organizations will be quarterly to allow for situational awareness across seasonal trends, a minimum level of continuity, and to establish a baseline of partnership among the members.

The Network's role in stewardship of crisis management activities for their department also means they have the ability to anticipate and respond to the needs of key stakeholders, they can manage expectations of local stakeholders responsibly and effectively, and they can connect with front-line operations as trusted partners.

Positioning Envoys across a Network in this way enables a faster, cleaner flow of relevant signals about issues – sometimes before these issues become crises. It also ensures that the core crisis team has faster access to early detection and better quality sensemaking in the initial phases of a real response.

This preparation leads to the second primary function for the Network: Response Coordination. As this book will explore later, organization for wide area or long duration responses calls for the creation of sub teams delegated from the central part of the response structure. The existence of the Network in blue sky conditions allows for much simpler and faster deployment of ad hoc, local structures to respond to escalating issues.

Those organizations that can build internal alliances and achieve coordination by sharing information and plans with external stakeholders prior to a crisis will experience greater success outcomes and less failure outcomes in crisis management than will those organizations lacking such alliances.[10]

In other words, as part of an integrated response framework, the Network should be considered available to support coordination of broad or regional responses, to participate in joint sensemaking, ongoing coordination calls and – perhaps most importantly – initial sizing up and escalation.

What happens when something happens?

Sometimes a crisis arrives with an unmistakable "bang." Other times the situation can be forecast to a certain extent – like a hurricane. And in yet other cases – such as the earthquake examples in the earlier chapter – the conditions on the ground are a matter of perception. Some felt the earthquake, while others felt nothing at all. And even when there is agreement on the fact that something has occurred, there may not be initial agreement as to what it means.

Crisis management research has shown over the years that the faster and more effective the initial recognition of a triggering event, the more likely the response will lead to favorable outcomes. This is the space where planning assumptions and on the ground reality first come into contact, and in most cases the distance between the two can be significant – even for the most well prepared organizations. As a result, having a size-up capability that is agile enough to handle the unexpected makes for far better outcomes in the final analysis.

Christine Pearson and Judith Clair presented a case for "multidimensional crisis management" in response to organizational crisis in their 1998 article, "Reframing Crisis Management." They concede that there is a role for crisis management in minimizing potential risk before it manifests itself, as discussed. But they also argue for a more agile response when the moment comes.

> "...In response to a triggering event, effective crisis management involves improvising and interacting by key stakeholders so that individual and collective sense making, shared meaning, and roles are reconstructed. Following a triggering event, effective crisis management entails individual and organizational readjustment of basic assumptions..."[11]

Their discussion shows what really happens when a crisis goes "bang." On a timeline from left to right, with a triggering event in the middle, there is only what was before, and what was after. In crisis management discussions, much emphasis is placed on left side activities, and the assumption that planning and preparation inevitably lead to better outcomes. What Pearson and Clair also note, however, is the role of perceptions of readiness before and after the event.

Every organization that participates in some level of planning will have attitudes and preconceived notions about its readiness for "crisis." These are informed by executive perceptions, cultural norms, as well as external factors like industry practices, regulatory considerations and institutionalized practices. However, when the triggering event occurs, it inevitably causes both *reactions* and *responses*.

The reactions occur on both an individual and a collective level and may take shape along the lines of denial and disbelief. "I can't believe this is happening," "This can't be happening to us." The effect of these shattered assumptions can be impaired emotional, cognitive, and behavioral performance.

However, the organizations that perform best in crisis management situations will shape a *response* (not just a reaction) to triggering events – both on an ad hoc and on a planned basis – that reflects three key characteristics:

1. Recognition that the triggering event has occurred. A shared acceptance of its existence.
2. A focus on making decisions early – practicing iterative leadership and getting a jump on the decision process.
3. Learning. Pearson and Clair recognize that the outcome of the triggering event will always be a combination of "success" and "failure," and that failure is to be expected in such circumstances.

"Sizing up" – recognizing the triggering event

This initial process of recognizing that something has happened or is happening, that some action may need to be taken, and some escalation may be necessary is commonly referred to as "sizing up."

As Pearson and Claire (among others, such as Arjen Boin) point out, the effectiveness of this initial recognition is what can separate an effective overall response from a less positive outcome. The significance of this activity should not be overlooked or taken for granted.

It is also worth pointing out that early recognition is not and cannot only be a centralized activity. In other words, the threat from inside or outside may start as a small, seemingly insignificant deviation. Having empowered, unbossed readiness-minded people throughout the organization – alongside a core team that is willing to listen to their concerns and act on their signals is critical. This is an opportunity for even complex organizations to *program* for readiness when the unexpected happens, whether their planning is relevant or not. Good sizing up also sets the stage for faster, bolder, more effective early decision-making. Nothing will aid the crisis team and the impacted operations more than leaders who are well-equipped to lead. A key part of that equation is a balanced picture of what the initial problem looks like.

There are several good processes and models for sizing up. For example, the Incident Command System, and variations on it, offer some great templates and baselines for "initial response phase" checklists.

The quintessential example of these is the ICS *Incident Briefing* ICS 201 Form. The intent of the 201 is to guide a formal process of collecting and reporting basic information about a situation, and to act as an initial action and resource allocation plan of sorts. The template asks the preparer to be explicit about what is happening, what immediate health or safety impacts may exist, and what the current and planned objectives are. All very reasonable and recommended steps – though perhaps somewhat challenging in the early stages. The templates also recommend that the preparer sketch or map the incident, assign strategies, define an organizational chart, list resources, etc. While perhaps helpful, some of these sections smack of a one size fits all approach which ICS critics commonly point to. It is also likely that in private sector, complex enterprise responses, these steps will not be relevant or needed in the immediate response phase. Unlike a kinetic incident like a major car accident or building collapse, where the situation can be at a surface level plain to the untrained eye, incidents in the business context may have less apparent impacts and risks.

It is also less likely that relationships between cause and effect will be as clear, or that the resources needed to address the situation will be as well understood or readily available. For example, a major traffic accident on a highway will likely require police, fire, and emergency medical services (EMS) response. Generally speaking, the types and availability of these resources are well understood to responders as a result of strong coordination among different agencies. It is also clear that a burning car requires fire apparatus to deal with the fire, EMS to deal with the human causalties, hazardous materials (HAZMAT) to handle any environmental impact, and police to secure the scene, handle traffic and participate in any investigation. The typing, direction and allocation of these resources is fairly straightforward and common across jurisdictions. In a business context, however, the response to the situation may be less obvious, and even if it is – the type, availability, and dispatching of needed resources may not be simple.

While the ICS structure offers some helpful ideas, there needs to be a model that underpins the sizing up process that can assist early recognition better so that time isn't wasted sketching scenes or assigning resources that can't be quantified. In other words, the ICS forms can be a useful tool for categorization and cataloging, but have limits as a *sensemaking* tool.

The good news is there are several models that support this activity, and which can be applied anywhere in an organization to guide sizing up and support sensemaking.

A habitat for crisis

One of these was created in 1999 by David Snowden who was at that time leading IBM Global Service's Knowledge and Differentiation Program. The model is known as the Cynefin Framework (pronounced *kuh-NEV-in*) and is described as a conceptual framework to aid in decision-making. The word "cynefin" comes from Welsh (Snowden himself is Welsh), and literally translates to *habitat* or *"a place for your multiple belongings."* According to Snowden,[12] the name implies that we are all rooted in multiple pasts which heavily influence what we are but of which we can only be partially aware. Thousands of variables influence all complex systems at any time – but we can only hope at best to partially perceive, understand, or process them. This is most definitely the case in an escalating crisis situation and is of paramount importance in the early detection of such a circumstance.

The model provides a single framework whereby leaders or decision makers can perceive viewpoints and integrate disparate concepts using a set of five contexts or domains. As we will see, however, the model need not only be a tool for leaders and decision makers.

When thinking about "sizing up" an incident or situation, the instinct may be to apply the classic 2 × 2 matrix commonplace to business and management consultancy for years. Something like this:

	Variable A	
	Low	High
Low		
High		

Variable B

Matrices like these are categorization models where the *framework* precedes the data. These models work very quickly in conditions where variables and data correspond, and the cause and effect relationships can be agreed upon and recognized easily. In those conditions, a 2×2 matrix can easily classify situations and guide optimized responses. In this way they are well suited to *exploitation* of available information.

What about conditions where the information is ... dodgy? What if instead of analysis there is speculation; instead of inputs there are gaps; instead of facts there are inconsistencies; instead of a "situation" there is a seemingly escalating series of circumstances; instead of constancy there is change?

In this case, what is needed is a model for *exploration* instead of *exploitation*. The Cynefin Framework is a very interesting model for thinking through these kinds of circumstances. When the data precedes the framework and patterns emerge through an iterative, almost social process, the model forms the basis for quick and effective sensemaking in practically any context.

The Cynefin Framework

Broadly, the framework presents systems which can be thought of as Ordered (or Predictable) and Unordered (or Unpredictable). Within these systems are the domains:

- **Clear** (also referred to as Obvious or "Simple")
  In this domain cause and effect relationships exist. They are understood and agreed upon, can be predicted and are repeatable. The conditions inside a Clear domain should be readily apparent to any reasonable observer.

  In this context, the recommended approach is to "sense-categorize-respond." This is to say, determine what the facts are (sense), categorize them, and respond accordingly. In this realm, best practices and standard operating procedures are common and work well, and probabilities can be depended upon.

Examples of activities in the Clear domains are following a recipe; procedural legal or regulatory matters; known scientific procedures like executing a simple chemical reaction; or mass production of a basic product. The ICS approach fits neatly into this domain.

- **Complicated**

In the Complicated domain, cause and effect relationships exist but are less immediately self-evident than in the Clear domain. It may be the case that some or most of the relevant variables are known or that what is needed is understood, but how to achieve it is not. These situations require either some kind of analytical method, expert advice, or both. In other words, the *what* is better understood than the *how* and a good result is likely with access to the right interpretation.

The recommended approach, therefore, is "sense-analyze-respond." The facts are established (sensed), experts or a method is used to analyze them, and a response is recommended. The key in this domain is that because analysis and an expert mindset are required, there will be several legitimate ways of getting to the "right" outcome. The caution often given in this domain is that because there can be a range of possible answers, insisting on a single correct path can serve to frustrate people – leaders, decision makers, and the expert analysts alike.

Examples of activities in the Complicated domain include: improving on an existing product; installing a building HVAC system (hiring expert contractors and installers to meet customer specifications); coaching a team (the rules of the game are understood, the players are known, but the winning strategy has to match the team and opponent's abilities).

- **Complex**

The system without causality is Complex. Cause and effect may be apparent only in hindsight, after the fact, and the outcomes are unpredictable on an emergent basis. If the circumstances were to be repeated and replayed with variables unchanged the outcomes could potentially be different each time.

The approach in these situations is "probe-sense-respond." As Arjen Boin said, "treat the problem as an experiment." Conduct experiments (probe), then amplify or dampen responses based on the results (sense) on an ongoing basis. Progress on the response can only be made in these settings by sensing and detecting patterns – and these patterns can only begin to emerge in response to action. The meaning of the word *cynefin* becomes apropos in this domain where non-linear relationships mean activities in one area can have outsized impacts in other areas – sometimes in surprising ways. Following the "probe-sense-respond" approach, stakeholders in these settings have to decide what is best because there can be no absolute right answer.

Examples of activities in the Complex domain include weather predictions; stock picking; poker playing; as well as human factors in complex business activities like leadership, developing trust, and changing a corporate culture.

- **Chaotic**

The Chaotic domain exists where the relationship between cause and effect cannot be determined, where probabilities have no value; or where variables cannot be identified or understood. In these conditions all responses will be considered novel in terms of the way things work – there is no basis for best practice, no precedent to depend upon, no immediate point of reference.

These conditions need to be stabilized quickly and immediate action called up so that the situation can be quickly transitioned to another domain. For that reason, the recommended approach is to "act-sense-respond." Think of a fire alarm going off in a building: the expectation is that building occupants stop what they are doing and immediately exit the building in an orderly fashion. This can be practiced so that the "act" is familiar, and we are all accustomed to the wait in the building parking lot while the "sense" is revealed. If there has been a true emergency, the situation is now "Complicated" and first responders will attend to the situation while the rest standby. On the other hand, if the alarm was a test and everyone can go back to work, then the all clear will be given and the situation is "Clear" or simple. Regardless of the outcome, in the moment when the alarm rings, the situation is temporarily "Chaotic" and requires immediate action.

Examples of Chaotic activities include war and battle situations or shocking new events. Interestingly, the Chaotic domain can be entered into deliberately. We think of this as innovation; disrupting industries with new technologies or services in ways that cannot be predicted is a strategy for some businesses.

One of the noteworthy aspects of the Cynefin framework is that it can also be used to assess responses to situations based on the observer's perspective.

- For instance, those who inhabit largely bureaucratic roles will be inclined to perceive problems as a failure of *process* in the Clear domain.
- A deep subject matter expert, on the other hand, will tend to view problems through the Complicated lens – seeing a failure of resources or analysis as the cause of a problem.
- There are also natural Complexity workers such as battlefield commanders and politicians who will react to situations by bringing together a range of perspectives hoping that one will arrive at a solution. These are often the best strategies.
- Lastly, the chaotic approach is the one in which a stakeholder's instinct is to seize total and unilateral control of the situation.

These tendencies can be thought of as preferences for action.

In the world of crisis management, much of the time is spent in the central space of the framework known as *disorder* where it is not yet known what domain we are in. Most situations will (and should) fall eventually into the Complex and Complicated domains. These domains offer the widest possible set of options for rapid and effective sensemaking –for fast recognition of a triggering event and movement into meaningful, iterative decision-making. These domains are complementary in many ways – and it is not important for those confronting an unstable situation to accurately identify their domain immediately. What is important, however, is to immediately recognize the presence of chaos. The next step is to acknowledge that the situation may need intervention by some relevant experts – either to diagnose (sense) the initial information or to aid in probing and sensing based on initial action (where more than one course of action may be appropriate and correct). More to follow on this.

Managing initial complexity – situational awareness in early response/pre-response

Using the Cynefin Framework, one may quickly determine that circumstances are neither Clear and Simple, nor Chaotic, and in doing so rule out the need for immediate actions and biases associated with those domains.

If the domain can be identified at all, is likely to reflect Complexity ("sense-analyze-respond") or Complication ("probe-sense-respond").

In either case, sizing up will involve the need for quick "sensing" of incoming signals – with or without the aid of experts or specialized methods. This is all part of the early sensemaking process that is known to lead to better overall outcomes.

Whether the situation is confronting experienced crisis practitioners, senior leaders, or frontline operations associates, it is always helpful to have a mental model to guide thought processes in a pinch. There are several of these in common practice: SIPDE, the OODA Loop, and of course PDCA (favored heavily by the ISO crowd).

In his book, *Blindsided: A Manager's Guide to Crisis Leadership*,[13] Bruce Blythe adapts the so-called SIPDE process to corporate crisis decision-making in corporate settings. SIPDE is adapted from the world of driver safety and is heavily preached in the motorcycle rider community where awareness of dynamic surroundings needs to be second nature.

Scan-Identify-Predict-Decide-Execute

SIPDE (which stands for Scan-Identify-Predict-Decide-Execute) is something we all do every day – especially when driving. For that reason, it also has easy applicability to the practice of initial size up – especially among non-crisis practitioners. The five steps of the SIPDE process are as follows:

- **Scan** the environment. The term commonly applied to this step is *situational awareness* or *vigilance* and is akin to the "sense" stage in the Cynefin approaches. In the context of driving, this is the normal pattern of observing the road ahead, having conscious awareness of what is on both sides of the vehicle, and checking the side and rearview mirrors. This is done to allow the driver to plan the path of travel and to connect with the environment immediately outside. Applied to emerging incidents, this means having the ability to build a jigsaw puzzle out of incomplete information, and with time constraints, in a way that considers the likelihood of escalation – or the "path of travel" – that the incident might take if it evolves.

- **Identify** potential problems in the scope of vision. These could be obvious or suspected – they could be seen from a distance or appear out of nowhere. For drivers this can mean stalled vehicles or debris in the lane on the highway; or an inattentive or distracted driver running a signal and entering the path of travel. The key in the Identify stage is that the observer is doing more than simply looking. They are engaging with their senses in a way that applies meaning to what they observe. This aligns both to the "sense" and "analyze" stages of the Cynefin approaches.

- **Predict** how those identified risks might manifest themselves, and what the menu of available options might be. In the driving example, this involves the almost subconscious process we all follow of reading the road, predicting other drivers' intentions, adapting our expectations according to changing traffic and weather conditions, etc. For those evaluating the early signs of potential crises, this means acknowledging the value in the intuitive sense operators will have of slight deviations in a system and how they might influence future performance. This is where the Cynefin framework shines in its recognition that there are more factors at play interacting with each other and the environment at any given time than any one person, team, or system can fully plan for. Nevertheless, the environment will offer signals to those who are capable of sensing and analyzing them – even on the fly.

- **Decide** what actions are needed, if any, based on the foregoing assessment. On the level of everyday driving, this takes place on an intuitive level as drivers naturally slow down, steer around, or otherwise avoid potential danger signs – ideally creating room for themselves and other drivers in the process. In the crisis management context, this involves thinking ahead about what decisions might be needed, and who will need to make those decisions. Specifically in the approach recommended in this book, the decisions are considered of value even if they turn out to be wrong. Many responses favor action – and even an informed decision that turns out to be the wrong one can be better than no decision at all. The process will result in better feedback in response to that action which will improve decisions in the future.

- **Execute** the decision. Do the thing that needs to be done. Steer the car, put on the brakes, and change lanes. Whatever the situation calls for. In the case of identifying a triggering event and sizing it up, the available options for action may be limited. It is likely that the only course of action – out of a few – may be to begin a rapid and responsible escalation. If that's the case, there should be little reason for delay, and little consequence for making a "wrong decision" to escalate. On the other hand, high consequence events occurring with low knowability and high uncertainty are by definition risky. Particularly for large, complex organizations it is vital to get the process started early and establish a common picture of what is happening.

The OODA Loop

Another important model for responding to initial complexity in a dynamic environment is the OODA Loop. Developed by Korean War-era US Air Force Colonel and military strategist John Boyd, the "OODA" in OODA Loop stands for Observe, Orient, Decide, Act. The idea originated with Boyd's observations concerning air to air combat between US F-86 Sabres and MiG15s in real world battle situations and his conclusion – based on his energy-maneuverability theory – that the pilot who could most quickly and capably respond to continuously changing conditions would prevail.

Boyd's idea was that all people (and organizations, as he later extended the concept) are in constant and continuous interaction with their environment. This interaction can be understood as a linear sequence of repeating activities.

- Observe – The collection of information using the senses.
- Orient – Forming a real time perspective based on these incoming signals; a rapid analysis.
- Decide – Determination of the best course of action based on that perspective.
- Act – Physically playing out the decision.

Then the Loop is repeated continuously. In its original formulation, the Loop was intended to aid fighter pilots in overcoming the overwhelming amount of incoming signals and data in the cockpit in order to make better decisions and ultimately get "inside" their opponents OODA Loop, thereby outmaneuvering them. Boyd theorized that by recognizing space and time from the cockpit appropriately, the relevance of certain data and therefore the number of decision options were slimmed down.

In the context of military strategy, there is a clear application, but the concept has since been incorporated into all sorts of realms from business strategy, marketing, litigation, and even play calling in football and basketball. On an individual level, one can practice the OODA Loop to engage with your surroundings and practice good situational awareness while driving or while walking through an unfamiliar city.

While the OODA Loop is frequently referred to in its tactical military and corresponding law enforcement contexts, there are some clear advantages to its applications in crisis management for complex organizations. One aspect of Boyd's work that is not often emphasized is his belief that the most effective organizations — be they governments, corporations, or the military — operated best when they decentralized their chains of command. That is to say, just as Von Moltke learned from Napoleon's experience, by using objective-driven orders (rather than highly specific method-driven ones), individual leaders and employees on the front lines can harness their own first-hand analysis and observation of the situation to drive better outcomes.

Boyd felt that traditional military Command and Control represented a top-down mentality that ignored or even stifled the actual, organic way in which humans behave and interact, especially when confronted with uncertainty stress and change. He preferred a paradigm where leaders shape or direct rather than "command." In this way, the "O" Observations and "O" Orientations that emerge from the operational level or front lines where the crisis is occurring can be appreciated and incorporated more quickly into strategic decision-making.

Build a clean container[14]

The rest of this book will talk about how to achieve the conditions where this phrase is possible. But as a practical matter, one of the most important initial steps in managing an emerging, unexpected crisis is to do what Jordan Strauss has called "building a clean container."

Assuming the organization has some level of crisis competency, some foundation in guiding principles, and has a minimum amount of blue sky preparation, the clean container idea can work pretty much anywhere. A clean container can be used both on the front lines and in the central operations center to establish initial sensemaking — to clarify the relevant factors and set up the organization for good initial decisions.

Think of the clean container as a blank sheet of paper. A blank ICS "201" form, flipped over to the other side. The back of an envelope. The back cover of the crisis management plan. It can be handwritten, done in a Word document, or an email. Whatever it is, the clean container will be organization specific.

Building a "clean container"

Phase 1 – size up

Recognize that you cannot anticipate everything; and that what happens next will not be perfect.

1. Be explicit about what is observed to be happening.
2. Be explicit about what the orientation or implication of this event is.
3. Return to first principles: what do we do every day and how is this different?
   a. Is the course of action clear or does it require immediate action? or
   b. Are there several possible ways to proceed based on an analysis we don't have? or
   c. Is there no basis for dealing with something like this because it is totally novel?
4. Establish how to intake and action information.
5. Determine when and how to escalate, if not already clear.

Phase 2 – response

Ask and answer the following questions:

1. Who's in Charge?
2. What needs to be done?
3. Who's doing what?

TAKEAWAY

Returning to the idea of sizing up, where circumstances are in "Complicated" or "Complex" domains, it is known that achieving an early and accurate picture of what is happening is critical to overall outcomes.

To manage this initial complexity or complication, there are a range of tools available on an organizational or individual level. What matters most is the following:

- Frontline operations must be trusted to recognize emerging patterns that deviate significantly from the norm.
- Front line managers must be trusted to orient to these patterns and begin to construct a recommendation independently.
- Senior leadership and the core crisis team must be responsive to these inputs and actively resist the tendency to increase friction or hinder interaction.

Notes

1. Paul C. Light, *Predicting Organizational Crisis Readiness: Perpectives and Practices Toward a Pathway to Preparedness.* The Center for Catastrophe Preparedness and Response (NYU) 24.
2. Ibid., p. 27.
3. Ibid., p. 29.
4. Ibid, p. 33.
5. Montgomery Van Wart and Naim Kapucu. "Crisis Management Competencies: The case of emergency managers in the USA," *Public Management Review* May 2011.
6. Ibid. p. 508 (Figure 4).
7. Paul C. Light, *Predicting Organizational Crisis Readiness: Perpectives and Practices Toward a Pathway to Preparedness.* The Center for Catastrophe Preparedness and Response (NYU)p. 55.
8. David Lindstedt, presentation May 15, 2014 "RPC Model of Organizational Recovery."
9. David Lindstedt and Mark Armour, *Adaptive Business Continuity* (Brookfield, CT: Rothstein Publishing), 2017,p. 37.
10. Christine M. Pearson and Judith A. Clair, "Reframing Crisis Management,"- Academy of Management Review, Vol. 23, No. 1, 1998, 59–76. From Arjen Boin, ed. Vol 2 Crisis Management, p. 18.
11. Ibid. From Arjen Boin, ed. Vol 2 Crisis Management, p. 10.
12. David Snowden, *The Cynefin Framework*, July 11, 2010 https://www.youtube.com/watch?v=N7oz366Xo-8
13. Bruce Blythe, *Blindsided: A Manager's Guide to Crisis Leadership* (Brookfield, CT: Rothstein Publishing), 2014, p. 42.
14. Jordan Strauss, Interview, November 2, 2021.

5

RAPID AND RESPONSIBLE ESCALATION

So far, this text has established that having a program of readiness that adopts planning but recognizes its potential limits is a good start. It has considered the possibility that crisis management need not be only a highly centralized activity, and it has recognized that bringing expertise to bear rapidly and recognizing triggering events quickly is key to managing crises… What next?

Declaring every possible problem a "crisis" and sending the organization into a response frenzy is not a strategy for success. On the other hand, establishing a process for recognizing triggering events and quickly establishing consensus around their possible implications is a strong bulwark against the "cry wolf" reflex. This is especially true in complex organizations when the problem detected at the edges can be framed or presented as an anomaly or an outlier. Calling attention to an anomaly is very different from "declaring an emergency" or labeling it a crisis. In fact, it is far more effective to frame complex problems as such because it attracts the right kind of attention from curious, solution-oriented experts. And those

DOI: 10.4324/9781003216803-7

are often the people who can most quickly place the anomaly in context – either as a non-issue or as a "triggering event."

This approach leads to a conversation around escalation. How and when should an organization escalate issues – and what process should they follow? This is one area that can benefit strongly from well-thought-out, documented, and rehearsed planning activity. A simple but strong, well-tailored incident escalation protocol will serve an organization as well on its own as any lengthy and detailed "crisis management plan."

This is also the point where storytelling and sensemaking begin to really pay off. To arrive at that point, one must consider two truths.

Planning for effects vs. planning for causes

The most important truth for crisis management planning is this:

> Regardless of cause, the effects of an incident will always only be the unexpected unavailability of people, places or things.[1]

In other words, there is an almost endless inventory of potential threats to an organization: natural disasters, man-made threats, accidents, etc. And each of these can be explored in extensive detail. Natural disaster planning could lead to hurricane planning, but hurricane plans need to be tailored to meet causes related to in-land flooding, coastal flooding, wind damage, and so on. A man-made threat could be categorized to include "terrorism." This can be further categorized to reflect the endless threats contained therein: armed attacks, man-portable IEDs, vehicle-borne IEDs, airborne attacks, chemical, biological, radiological, etc.

The scope of possible causes of crisis is only limited by the imagination – and can lead to ceaseless and futile planning, even when these are ranked according to likelihood or overall risk. The reason is simple. Regardless of what causes the circumstances, the organization will be confronted with the same limited effects: the loss of staff, the loss of facilities, or the loss of resources.

From a planning perspective, does it ultimately matter whether a critical facility was unexpectedly taken offline because it was destroyed by a fire, lost to a flood, or invaded by ghosts? The effect will be the same: the critical activities at that location will be unavailable until it can be restored or replaced. The organization has no control over the weather, human adversaries, or super-natural forces. But it *can* be ready for the effects of unexpected losses.

What this means, in all seriousness, is that focusing energy on improving response and recovery capabilities that are in one's control matters most. The traditional approach of focusing all-hazards preparedness externally can be limiting and – at times – wasteful. The notion of focusing internally as well on the locations, people, and resources that have the most direct bearing on critical processes leads to much more valuable planning and readiness activity.

Flavors of response

The next truth to recognize is that there are many different manifestations of crises, each with its own "flavor" or idiosyncrasy of response. Many things differentiate these crises and their associated responses, but key among them are the characteristics of "pace and place."[2] That is, temporal and spatial dimensions of the crisis mean they are typically recognized as fast burning or slow burning situations. Fast burning crises have a clear beginning and end, and will match with commonly recognized concepts of what a crisis is. Slow burning crises, on the other hand, simmer and incubate for longer periods of time. They can remain undefined or poorly defined and even change character over time – generating regular surges of activity, but without ever really reaching closure.

Fast burning crises

- **"Simple problems" at complex organizations**
  Sometimes large enterprises have a tendency to bring so much complexity to bear on a problem that the circumstances take on a life of their own. This is a bureaucracy at its finest – where the process required to solve the problem is treated as far more important than the problem, its solutions, or any of the people involved in the matter. This is the kind of environment that *Unboss* was created in opposition to. The recognition that an organization's own peculiar problem solving approach could amplify the problem is an important distinction. Unfortunately, these can sometimes be the hardest trajectories to change – and are sometimes the most difficult for teams to recognize

or admit to themselves. In retrospect, these are often seen as self-inflicted crises where a problem occurred but "the institution allowed it." This is how General Duane Deal from the Shuttle Columbia disaster investigation board summarized that event, "The (insulating) foam did it... the institution allowed it."

- **Emerging risks**

  Risks that are new or newly recognized do not have features which are well understood or fully contemplated. Their effects are hard to quantify, and as a result their impact on the organization cannot be placed properly into context. It can also be the case that such risks are rapidly evolving, or represent a new combination of risks – adding to their lack of wide understanding or acceptance. As such their broad impacts, associated costs and optimal strategies for management can only be theorized. For crisis management practitioners and their clients, these conditions lie in the Complex or Complicated Cynefin domains. They require more time, knowledge, and specialized expertise to handle. For example, many will acknowledge that climate change is an emerging risk. The potential for fast burning crises arising out of this risk may lie in the potential for new or unusual acute weather patterns, such as tornados occurring in areas not normally prone to them; or the impacts of wildfires on energy utility operations in the Western US.

- **Reputational or institutional crises**

  These are any event which can threaten the perceptions held by stakeholders, or damage the good name or standing of an organization in its community. The greatest threat posed by reputational risks is that they can be hidden dangers. These crises can be brought about by the overt actions of a company; but they can also just as easily arise indirectly through the actions of employees, for example, or as a result of real or perceived connections to third parties, such as joint venture partners or suppliers. This is an area where a centrally led, tightly coordinated crisis response makes sense. But it should also be noted that because of their stealthy nature, reputational crisis can become a feature of other incidents – perhaps even seemingly innocuous ones. The core crisis team should remain alert to this, and be prepared to intervene with a centrally coordinated response where appropriate. Examples of fast-burning reputational crises may include the responses to the Volkswagen emissions scandal and the Takeda airbag recalls.

Slow burning crises

- **Long crises**

  The extended, protracted responses that consist of the accumulation of many smaller battles and monopolize the attention of resources or organizations for long periods of time. Examples include epidemics, the Great Depression, and World Wars I and II. These crises often occur on a global or society-wide scale, such that the effects are felt across many organizations, industries, or geographies. The "living companies" have found the way through these crises – as discussed earlier – by staying committed to the bigger picture. They stay true to their values, remain willing to alter direction, and honor and reward the ability of their people to grow and adapt. For crisis management practitioners, the long crisis will be exhausting and all-consuming. To succeed they will need to fight the smaller battles one at a time, while keeping perspective on the larger vision for the organization in the long run.

- **"Creeping crises"[3]**

  The "creeping crisis" is "… a threat to widely shared societal values or life-sustaining systems that evolves over time and space, is foreshadowed by precursor events, subject to varying degrees of political and/or societal attention, and impartially or insufficiently addressed by authorities…"[4] In other words, the creeping crisis comes on slowly, will eventually reach some critical mass or tipping point, and will often be viewed only in retrospect as inevitable. What is uniquely insidious about these situations is that aspects of the problem will be apparent to most, but the will to action or intervention is not present until it is too late – or almost too late. These problems are most often political or global in nature. Examples may include the COVID-19 response, the debate concerning climate change, and the acknowledgment or response to human rights violations and genocide globally.

Putting it into practice

For the purposes of readiness, first set aside the discussion around all potential causes of disaster. What matters first is establishing the basis for a rapid and responsible escalation in response to the triggering event, whatever it may be. Ensure that planning focus is not monopolized by the specifics of given risk events. Instead, focus internally on the effects that matter:

- How will people and staff be ready and attend to their critical needs?
- If critical facilities are lost or compromised, what steps need to be taken?
- If key resources are unexpectedly unavailable, what needs to be done?

Focus planning on these questions first. Then consider causes through the lens of "flavors of response" – without going through the inventory of everything that can possibly go wrong.

The approach should be to focus on:

- Detecting anomalies. Have a culture that values detecting and reporting them.
- Assessing anomalies. Have the ability to recognize if an anomaly is dangerous, if there is a method for dealing with it, or if there is a need for expertise to assess in more detail.
- To the extent practical, setting realistic triggers or tripwires for escalation.
- Addressing the issues with speed, accuracy and transparency.

The outcome of this review can be a protocol for rapid escalation that is tailored to the organization.

Here is an example of what this can look like (Figure 5.1):

Notice the features of this example:

- **The protocol fits on one page.**
  This is not a detailed procedure; rather it is a simple aide to memory, or a mnemonic device meant to prompt common sense responses.
- **It is not prescriptive.**
  It does not say, "When threshold X is reached on critical process Y initiate SOP 123." Instead the protocol uses examples of situations that would match each escalation level. These examples are necessarily highly specific to the organization – perhaps even to the business unit or the geography in question.

Organizational Rapid Escalation Protocol

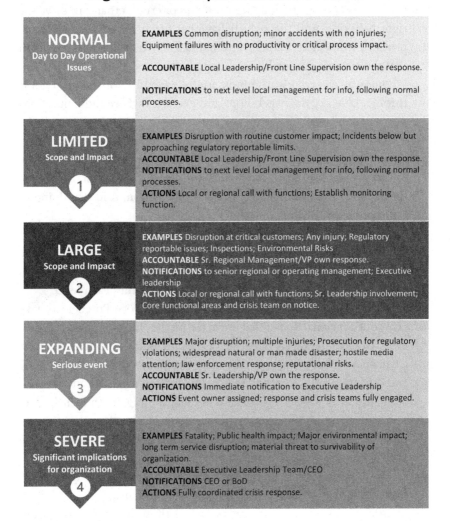

NORMAL
Day to Day Operational Issues

EXAMPLES Common disruption; minor accidents with no injuries; Equipment failures with no productivity or critical process impact.

ACCOUNTABLE Local Leadership/Front Line Supervision own the response.

NOTIFICATIONS to next level local management for info, following normal processes.

LIMITED
Scope and Impact
1

EXAMPLES Disruption with routine customer impact; Incidents below but approaching regulatory reportable limits.
ACCOUNTABLE Local Leadership/Front Line Supervision own the response.
NOTIFICATIONS to next level local management for info, following normal processes.
ACTIONS Local or regional call with functions; Establish monitoring function.

LARGE
Scope and Impact
2

EXAMPLES Disruption at critical customers; Any injury; Regulatory reportable issues; Inspections; Environmental Risks
ACCOUNTABLE Sr. Regional Management/VP own response.
NOTIFICATIONS to senior regional or operating management; Executive leadership
ACTIONS Local or regional call with functions; Sr. Leadership involvement; Core functional areas and crisis team on notice.

EXPANDING
Serious event
3

EXAMPLES Major disruption; multiple injuries; Prosecution for regulatory violations; widespread natural or man made disaster; hostile media attention; law enforcement response; reputational risks.
ACCOUNTABLE Sr. Leadership/VP own the response.
NOTIFICATIONS Immediate notification to Executive Leadership
ACTIONS Event owner assigned; response and crisis teams fully engaged.

SEVERE
Significant implications for organization
4

EXAMPLES Fatality; Public health impact; Major environmental impact; long term service disruption; material threat to survivability of organization.
ACCOUNTABLE Executive Leadership Team/CEO
NOTIFICATIONS CEO or BoD
ACTIONS Fully coordinated crisis response.

Figure 5.1 Example of a rapid escalation protocol.

There is a role here for coordination between the central crisis management team, local management, and Crisis Champions to calibrate the examples in the protocol correctly. This is most important in the lower escalation levels of the protocol. It should be clear what differentiates a normal day-to-day problem from a full blown crisis. But the delineation between Normal and Limited; or between Limited and Large; could be subject to interpretation.

It is critically important that teams examine the borders between these areas closely and identify examples or criteria that will drive the right behavior. And the right behavior is for anyone referring to the protocol to escalate without any hesitation – or to be *very* confident that the current protocol level is appropriate.

One way to arrive at the most useful examples for the protocol is through blue sky day workshops and exercises where these questions are put to the test.

Above all, the intent is that the user on the front lines in operations – where the problems often begin – can be assured that the reference to this protocol is meant to encourage them to take action, to escalate to the next level even without perfect information. And that doing so will not be punishable.

- **An accountable role is pre-identified.**

To the extent that it is possible, alignment should occur during blue sky planning in advance so that it is understood who will be in charge – at least initially – during the transition into each level.

There is no reason for a CEO or even Senior Vice President to take charge of a regional matter that might fall on the "Large" level in this protocol. In actuality, this is often the case – and senior executives can have a tendency or feel a duty – to take charge in matters that are more rightly and ably managed at local and regional levels. Getting clarification on this at the planning stage is a good idea. In that planning, it can be helpful to seek agreement on the primacy of local leadership under certain conditions. At the same time, balance the need for updates and information with a step that includes commitment to notification to senior leaders.

On the other hand, there can be issues so severe that the senior-most leadership needs to take immediate command. This is without question. However, circumstances such as those are impossible not to recognize. Part of the advantage of using a protocol like this is to help address smaller anomalies or creeping concerns before they become crises. And to be ready if they do.

- **The first action is always notification.**

To drive these behaviors, the protocol commits to notification or communication as a first step at each level, with subsequent actions to follow. Typically, further internal communication is a next best step, such as establishing an incident call.

- **Escalation goes both ways.**

  Just as one should not hesitate to escalate issues up, the organization can use this protocol to recognize the truth about all incidents. Whatever the case may be, situations will always have a tendency to expand and contract over time, using more and different types of resources (and the ability to manage them) in the process. In other words, just as the situation escalates up, it will also deescalate back down eventually. Part of ensuring rapid and responsible escalation is allowing a response to flex up quickly but without creating chaos, so that it can relax back down just as easily without leaving everyone feeling like a "cry wolf" has just been called.

- **It is a living document.**

  A protocol like this cannot be considered finalized. As a reference, or guidance, it should be understood as subject to interpretation, change, and updating. The learning organization puts a protocol like this into practice with some testing and trial, but mostly adapts it through meaningful real-world experience.

  These changes should be iterative, building upon and improving the protocol – making it work better in an organic way. But it should not be subject to changes that are so frequent or seemingly arbitrary that it loses value or credibility. Instead, the protocol should reflect the voice and conscience of the end users, balanced with the needs and expectations of leaders at various levels.

Simple, but not easy: recommendations for implementing a protocol

Unconquerable organizations do rapid, responsible escalation well, but it isn't easy for every company. Part of the reason is cultural. Unconquerable, living companies trust their people, relate to their communities; know their place in the world; and don't live in fear of external forces. They have a healthy relationship with their critical stakeholders, and they include local frontline workers and leaders among their critical stakeholders.

The example protocol included here is nothing but an outline. The real thing needs to be highly customized to the organization where it is applied. Some organizations will prefer numbers, other colors, different languages, and so on.

There is a pitfall in such exercises where the protocol can begin to resemble the old "threat levels" of early Homeland Security days in the years following 9/11. Part of the problem with national-level protocols like that is they lack specificity, reinforce ambiguity, and often seem arbitrary to the end users. Those outcomes should be avoided.

Where practical, an escalation protocol should be highly specific to a community of workers or teams because it originates in part from their input. It should remain simple and straightforward, reinforcing immediate common sense expectations, and allowing the organization to meaningfully bend and flex to circumstances that may defy easy explanation.

The features of an effective protocol include:

- Concise. One page. Visually appealing.
- Non-prescriptive. Driven by examples, relatable references. Not an SOP.
- Accountable owner is identified by role (not by name) at each level.
- Communication/notification is always the first escalation step.
- There should be an understanding that the protocol can be quickly escalated up as the incident worsens, but also that the protocol can be quickly escalated down if conditions turn out to be less severe than they appeared initially. There should be an expectation that escalation in either direction should not create chaos among the team. Most especially, it should be clear that there are no negative consequences for workers who raise the level.

Consider this worksheet version of the protocol (Figure 5.2) with some key questions for developing and applying locally:

To illustrate this concept further, consider how a response protocol could be applied to each of the flavors of response to improve identification of a triggering event, and facilitate a better response.

"Simple problems" at complex organizations – don't fight the power (all at once)

The organization may be its own worst enemy either because its own internal bureaucracy is creating the problem or is making the problem worse. The challenge for response protocols in these contexts is twofold.

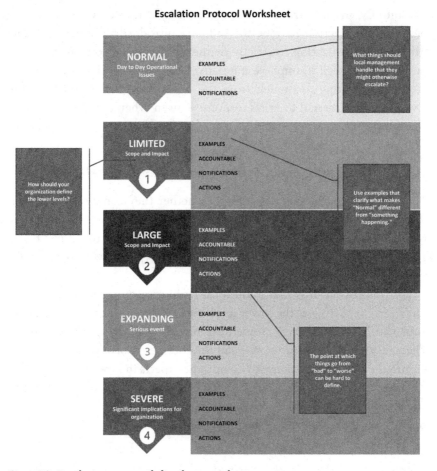

Figure 5.2 Escalation protocol development key questions.

First, the escalation protocol creators will have to overcome a strong tendency on the part of the organization to turn it into a prescription or standard operating procedure. Reference documents that are treated as guidelines sometimes seem to carry less authority than weightier policy counterparts.

The second challenge will be to deal with under- or over-escalating. In other words, workers in this setting may feel reluctant to set organizational wheels in motion without significant confidence in the presence of an anomaly. Alternately, they may respond by escalating everything and battering level-up management with insignificant concerns.

Candidly, in organizations characterized by extreme bureaucracy, the best course of action may be to gradually introduce a simple protocol. Allow the organization to strictly define its response protocol in elaborate detail but seek to improve it iteratively by showing the value of less-is-more. Deviating too much from the prevailing culture too fast will always be detrimental to crisis response – even when that culture needs changing.

Emerging risks – don't hesitate to escalate

The challenge with emerging risks is whether they come on quickly or slowly, they don't offer any point of reference. In these cases, the first report will never look like the last due to the fact that the context and analysis needed to properly understand them is typically not immediately available.

For this reason, it is important for a rapid escalation protocol to reinforce early reporting at the lower levels. Minor deviations in complex systems can have unexpected, sometimes rapidly amplifying consequences. The detection of these early on – and the routine reporting of them – can ensure the practiced response of competent experts in rare moments when the issue turns out to be of significance. If the issue turns out to be a true emergent risk, the time advantage given to decision makers and strategists by early identification and reporting will be valuable.

Reputational or institutional crises – do the right thing

These issues can take the form of other flavors, like emerging risks or creeping crises, and they can come just as quickly from the external environment with a bang as they can from deep down in the operational depths.

In escalating matters related to reputational or core institutional topics, the organization depends on its core values. A culture of speaking up and of psychological safety is important to making sure these concerns are properly heard in time to do anything about them. This ultimately comes down to ethics and providing managers and employees with the assurance that they are expected to do the right thing; that they won't be ridiculed, punished, or retaliated against for doing so. There is a lot depending on, and a lot expected of employees and their managers in these scenarios.

Long crises – it's a marathon, not a sprint

These crises are characterized by many smaller sub-incidents or campaigns. The organization navigating a long crisis will find itself at any given point in the midst of a subplot of the much larger story that is happening to society. In the example of COVID-19, the spring of 2020 was characterized by the very sudden, acute phase of the pandemic and the business world's adaptation to remote work on a vast scale. Subsequent chapters of the COVID-19 long crisis involved the early vaccine deployment; the transition between Federal Administrations; the impact of variants and so on. Within any of these phases, individual organizations will be confronted with unique challenges (how to respond to an increasingly vaccinated population; changes in regulatory requirements; commercial property management; and workforce business continuity, etc). The ability to continuously practice detection, response, and escalation becomes exhausting, but no less important to seeing the matter through long term.

"Creeping crises" – don't say I told you so

The thing about a creeping crisis is… well… it creeps, and no one really pays attention to it until it is too late. In a perfect world, a great rapid response protocol would enable organizations to detect and escalate the deviations before they become destabilizing. But in actuality, these kinds of situations defy identification as problems worth solving and they remain ignored until they reach a critical stage.

Consequently, the best one can hope for is to accelerate the response when the moment does arrive. Here the challenge will also be to resist the urge to say, "I told you so." The protocol can help by defining the who, what, and when of the response.

Important considerations for escalation

As one moves through the protocol the incident is necessarily expanding in some way. It will require more and different kinds of resources and the ability to manage them. This is the case for every flavor of response, and it is worth considering when constructing an escalation protocol.

- Delegation – At every level of a protocol, and in every response from the normal day-to-day problem to large, escalating and severe crises some delegation needs to take place. The more delegation that can be done, to the lowest reasonable level, the better. By the time an incident reaches a certain level of severity, a team of people should already be engaged. The best way to coordinate activities is to ensure that delegation is allowed, understood as part of the process, and the delegation of tasks and authority is understood to be a key responsibility of the accountable person.

- Keeping Track − The protocol can serve as a trigger for starting this process early. Doing so can be very helpful, and it need not be elaborate or highly detailed. Recordkeeping should be baked in from the initial notification onward. At the earliest stages, record keeping and tracking actions is not the most critical priority. This is where the *clean container* comes in. Keep it simple now, so it can be kept simple later. If an incident escalates to a significant level of severity the ability to quickly status actions in progress vs actions completed will become critical.

  At first, some of the key facts to track are the basic sequence of events in a simple timeline; who the responding stakeholders are; and the answers to several key questions as the basis of a situation report.

These are some of the questions to keep in mind as an incident advances through the protocol:

- **What is taking place that shouldn't be?**
- **What is not happening that should be?**
- **What else will have to happen for this to escalate further?**

For example, in the context of operations consider questions such as:

- Signals: Are there inconsistencies between normal equipment readings? Or, are sensors or data sources not responding or providing data?
- Causality: Are actions taken not resulting in normal or expected outcomes?
- Communications: Is there an increase/decrease in the normal pattern of messaging?
- Other significant deviations.

"Tweeners": the key escalation points: from 0 to 1, and from 1 to 2...

In the example protocol provided here there are two critical points that represent the most common source of failure in early recognition and rapid, responsible escalation.

These can be seen as the transitions or gaps between "Normal" and "Limited" in this example; and the transition from "Limited" to "Large." Think of these kinds of incidents as the in-betweeners, "The Tweeners."

As we have discussed, early recognition leads to better outcomes and wins the day. Recognizing a problem is easy when it is so serious it can't be ignored. These are the kinds of issues that immediately present at Expanding or Severe crises on this sample protocol. An explosion, an armed assault, a building collapse, and a catastrophic natural disaster. These are all the macro events that the organization cannot fail to recognize.

The real challenge – and the real risk of failure – occurs on the opposite end of the spectrum. Not differentiating between normal business operations and a deviation with potential to create harm can lead to an issue quietly expanding unnoticed until it reaches a more obviously problematic level. At this later stage, the response can still be successful, but the harm may be greater, and the accompanying stakes are much higher than they could have been with earlier intervention.

The first escalation level is the most important. But what kinds of things prevent responsible escalation at this level? There can be many reasons: cultural, time-pressure related, competitive pressures, resourcing limitation, or any combination of these and other factors.

For this reason, it is critical that the protocol be organizationally and operationally specific. Simply applying a template will not improve outcomes – especially at this level.

Lead a "Pre-mortem" exercise

In deploying escalation protocols, one of the first and best steps to take is to exercise the proposed escalation in a workshop with operations leads, workers, and their supervisors. The intent is not to test their knowledge or put them on the spot, but rather to bend and break a protocol into something that will work for them on the frontline level. Think of this as the opposite of an After-Action Review. It is a Before-Action Review or a "pre-mortem." This is especially helpful in clarifying confusion or disagreement in the "tweener" areas between escalation levels.

Experience with these types of exercises shows a couple of common discussion points that can emerge:

- First, it provides an opportunity for local and central leadership to collectively demonstrate support for developing a protocol that serves the front lines.
  - It conveys the truth that such a protocol depends on frontline input.
  - The exercise creates an opportunity for operational players to become familiar with the intent, objective, and visual/organizational shape of such a protocol.
  - Identify the right language to describe levels, if Normal, Limited, Large, etc. aren't relevant words to describe levels.
  - Clarify the scope of what areas the protocol will apply to.
- Second, a workshop or exercise will challenge the participants to reach a consensus on what the escalation points should look like by defining a set of examples at each level.
  - Some examples may be obvious or predefined, such as regulatory reporting trip wires. The purpose instead is to clarify the more subjective, but equally important areas.
  - Identify the "Tweeners" from the equivalent of Normal to Limited, and from Limited to Large.
  - Establish that the examples provided are for illustration purposes and that they should be things that prompt the right action among the operations team. Then collect meaningful, specific examples at each level.
- Lastly, the team may want to confront a scenario that falls in the "Tweener" category as an example. Something that frontline operations could handle but which could have the potential to expand. An issue that could go either way. Ideally, the outcome of the discussion is clarity around the expectations for when and how to escalate – and that doing so will not be punishable at the edges of the organization. Provided it is done responsibly, and not as a means of passing the buck up on everything.

This is a difficult balance to strike, clearly, and is fundamental to management practice. However, it is raised here as an area worth focusing attention on. The seams between the early levels of a response protocol can be the most difficult to define and act on and that should be acknowledged. Incidents that rise to a certain level of severity and stop or do not seem to escalate further can create disagreement over the decision not to escalate. This is perfectly understandable, and a normal human instinct.

Part of the task is to create trust and equilibrium between leadership teams and frontline operations so that each can handle the tasks appropriately given to them. Unbossed teams will tackle issues head-on, innovate solutions, and find a way through. But they are also trusted to be responsible for keeping those elsewhere in the organization informed on matters that can have a wider impact. By the same token – these unbossed, frontline workers and teams are the ones often best placed to detect the critical anomalies that could easily be ignored but wind up being enormously consequential. A protocol can provide the venue for these people to ensure their concerns get heard – early and in the proper context.

The properly calibrated escalation protocol will define impact thresholds for teams, drive adaptive leadership and clarify strategic and tactical priorities down the line if escalation patterns continue.

Early response imperatives

One aspect of the "responsible" part of rapid and responsible escalation has to do with doing the right things first, and keeping the big picture in mind. This can be hard to do in the heat of the moment.

One way to address this challenge is to establish a set of early response imperatives. Generally speaking, these are already well recognized in the emergency management and response communities. In order of importance, the first three things that any situation or potential emergency/crisis demand are the following:

1. Ensure life safety.
2. Establish incident stability.
3. Conserve the environment and protect property to the extent practical.

Ensuring life safety is always the first priority. If there is a risk of injury or a severe safety concern, this needs to be addressed before anything else. The lives in question include not only potential victims of an emergency, but also workers, the public, and any responders themselves. There is no sense in running into a burning building to rescue victims if the rescuers themselves become victims – thereby immediately escalating the situation further.

Incident stability can be an overlooked factor in private sector response, but it is a priority that is well articulated under the ICS system. This term refers to the need to have the right resources to manage the situation *and* the ability to manage them. Seeking incident stability should be a key priority for core crisis teams in complex organizations because they often are better able to bring resources to bear than local teams alone (who should be focused on the local matter primarily). Nevertheless, the key here is that not having enough resources to manage a situation can be just as bad as having too many resources without the ability to manage and coordinate them. Blue sky planning that aligns Crisis Champions with the Core team and management at multiple levels helps clarify this problem and its potential solutions. Applying a well-thought-out response escalation protocol which identifies accountable roles at each level, and a clear communication line upward, is the best first step to defining stability.

The imperative to protect property and the environment follows. This serves to ensure that protection of the environment is considered a top priority and given due attention in responses – not overshadowed by other considerations after life safety and stability are established. It also serves as a reminder that property and environmental consideration – while important – should never take precedence over human life or the ability to bring practical measures to bear in containing the incident.

TAKEAWAYS

The most important truth for crisis management planning is this: Plan for Effects, Not Causes.

> Regardless of cause, the effects of an incident will always, only be the unexpected unavailability of people, places, or things.

The second truth is that crises take many specific shapes and forms. Some come on fast (Simple Problems at Complex Organizations, Emerging Risks, and Reputational/Institutional Crisis); and others come on slowly (Long Crises and Creeping Crises). However, regardless of cause, and regardless of "flavor," the early recognition and action on a triggering event will result in better outcomes if things get worse. To program for this kind of readiness, a tailored but adaptive escalation protocol can serve an organization well. These protocols should prioritize detecting, assessing, and escalating anomalies with speed and accuracy – without sending the organization into routine chaos.

This approach can be practiced and improved over time with good blue-sky planning and "premortem" exercises, while always keeping in mind the key response imperatives: first protect life, then stabilize the incident, then protect property/environment. All other actions flow from there.

Notes

1. See AdaptiveBCP.org
2. Arjen Boin, Magnus Ekengren, and Mark Rhinard, "Hiding in Plain Sight: Conceptualizing the Creeping Crisis," Risks, Hazards & Crisis in Public Policy, Vol. 11, No. 2, 2020.
3. Arjen Boin Interview; and Arjen Boin, Magnus Ekengren, and Mark Rhinard, Risks, "Hiding in Plain Sight: Conceptualizing the Creeping Crisis," Hazards & Crisis in Public Policy, Vol. 11, No. 2, 2020.
4. Ibid p. 122.

PART III

6

THE ONLY THREE QUESTIONS YOU NEED TO ASK – WHO'S IN CHARGE – CRISIS LEADERSHIP

Unconquerable organizations know crises can take many forms but share common characteristics. They appreciate that early recognition paired with rapid responsible escalation can help contextualize responses.

What, then, is the best way to address a properly identified "crisis" when it materializes? How can this be achieved while keeping a connection between the edges of the organization and a central guiding team?

In other words, something is definitely happening. Now what?

When it comes right down to it, there are really only three questions that need to be asked and answered in any crisis:

- *Who's in charge?*
- *What needs to be done?*
- *And who's doing what?*

These are the basis for an unconquered response when crisis hits.

The ability to ask and answer these basic questions is the first step in moving toward responsible escalation, incident stability, and effective

DOI: 10.4324/9781003216803-9

response. More simply and at a high level, if one cannot ask and answer these three questions, then no further action should be taken until they can be addressed. The questions should be answerable at any point in a response – not only at the beginning or the end.

Broadly, these questions address the core elements of good crisis response: crisis leadership, action and resource management, and the role of the crisis team and other responders. This section of the book will look at each of these core elements in turn.

As part of that review, it is helpful to keep in mind the simple response management elements which have begun to come together in the earlier parts of this book.

- Point 1: Rapid Responsible Escalation
- Point 2: Sensemaking – What's the Story Being Told Here?
- Point 3: Bold Effective Decision Making
- Point 4: Action

Readiness is in large part a function of culture. Good readiness culture, which is supportive of the whole organization, is expressed in meaningful Guiding Principles. These can be organization-wide, or defined with a specific crisis management context if that's more appropriate. Guiding principles can be refined through blue-sky training and exercising – all of which also aid in developing trust across the organization and reinforcing the readiness vision.

One of the most important guiding principles involves enabling the edges of the organization: pushing sole responsibility for decision making from the center alone, to the periphery, and resisting the urge to centralize power and decision making. Through this principle, an organization creates the conditions where people can adapt, based on their experience and expertise, and inform the overall decision making and response process. This approach requires teams and groups to talk to one another and take responsibility.

Walmart and Hurricane Katrina

The aftermath of Hurricane Katrina in New Orleans and the greater US Gulf Coast region in August of 2005 was unquestionable devastation. In the years to follow, the local, state, and federal authorities accountable for leading the response were heavily criticized for a disjointed and uncoordinated recovery effort. Meanwhile, a lesser known success story was a heroic response led by local Walmart managers on the ground in Louisiana as part of a loosely coordinated effort by the company as a whole.

In advance of the storm's arrival, Walmart had already begun the delivery of nearly 2500 truckloads of merchandise to its stores in the impacted area, and had drivers and a transport network in place to ship relief supplies to community members in the area, in partnership with local aid agencies. This was all part of their existing readiness planning and culture. In the immediate aftermath of the storm, 126 Walmart Stores and two distribution points were closed. Some had lost power, others were flooded and many reported damage. Within 10 days all but the 15 most heavily damaged of these locations were back open and operating.

The reason Walmart was able not only to recover its own infrastructure so quickly, but also to take a leading role in helping restore the community around it, is the significant amount of latitude and discretion it gives frontline workers.

As the storm approached, Walmart CEO Lee Scott issued a famous edict to his senior staff, with the direction to cascade it down their lines of command to regional, district, and store-level managers.

The message was simple, clear, and succinct. "This company will respond to the level of this disaster," Scott said. "A lot of you are going to have to make decisions above your level. Make the best decision that you can with the information that's available to you at the time, and, above all, do the right thing."[1]

This is a perfect example of "commander's intent" deployed and put into action by frontline leaders. This message was understood by Walmart's frontline workers in the impacted areas, and implemented. In several cases, store managers allowed local residents or emergency responders to take needed supplies from Walmart stores – with and without manager approval. In some cases they even fashioned crude paper-slip credit systems to track resource movements. In Kenner, Louisiana, a worker used a forklift to access bottled water supplies in a damaged warehouse so responders could deliver them to a retirement home. Elsewhere in Louisiana, Walmart stores were used as command centers and sleeping quarters for police officers and first responders. In a Mississippi store, the local manager used a bulldozer to access the damaged store to retrieve vital medicines from the pharmacy and critical supplies from the shelves. In these cases, Walmart management and executives praised the actions of these workers.

What is evident is that the company's executives trusted their workers enough to give them bold, broad guidance and know that they would do the right thing. What is also evident is that leadership in crisis occurs at many levels. In this case, the CEO and executive team took their crisis leadership role seriously. But so did many other individuals from district to store levels – people for whom "crisis response" is probably not normally in their job description. How was this possible?

- Walmart executives were faster than most to recognize what was happening as a complex problem (in the Cynefin sense of the word), and that a tightly controlled centralized approach would fail.
- They immediately delegated authority down to the most reasonable levels, while escalating information up only as far and fast as needed.
- They prioritized communication over instruction – and made sure people talked to each other, locally. Judgment was valued (and expected) over instruction or procedure. There was no SOP for the things they did or needed to do. The response needed to be dictated by the conditions on the ground and the assessment by those present.
- They established objectives that were practical and driven by their values. Walmart employees were to first ensure their own safety and the safety of their families; they would then support responders and relief agencies, while also restoring company infrastructure.

This is a rare and exceptional performance, held against the backdrop of a widespread disaster and lacking government response. But perhaps it doesn't have to be. This level of capability is within the reach of any organization with the will to achieve it.

Who's in charge: crisis leadership

The fact remains that when crisis strikes, the readiness – just like the plans – will only be as good as the team that confronts the situation. Good teams require leadership; but when crisis strikes, those leaders who cannot or will not relinquish sole control in a complex situation are most likely to fail. The unconquerable organization needs the right kind of leadership.

You are trusted to know what the right thing to do is. And you are expected to do it. In essence, this was Lee Scott's message to the Walmart executive team. That team then echoed the message down from each level of management to the next in a huge organization – straight down to the store level. They achieved an astonishing outcome by leveraging the power of their people.

What does it take to deliver leadership in other than normal circumstances? What are the elements of crisis leadership that serve responding organizations best? Where does leadership in crisis come from, and how can leadership become "ready" for service in real-world responses? How can crisis leaders achieve better outcomes by empowering the edges of the organization and reining in complexity?

This chapter will explore what crisis leadership is and what it does. What follows are ideas to provoke debate and thought about how crisis leadership can work. Admittedly, this is not a book solely dedicated to crisis leadership – the hope is to provide ideas and inspiration which can be brought to bear in thinking about what makes good crisis leadership, and a few of the practical aspects of it at a strategic and operational day-to-day level.

What is crisis leadership?

What does it mean to lead in crisis? In other-than-normal business conditions (what the Cynefin framework would consider *Complicated* or *Complex*), other than normal leadership is required. These are conditions in which the relationship between cause and effect is not – or cannot – be known; where more data adds to the problem rather than leads to a solution; and where existing frameworks cannot bring clarity or stability to the situation. The answer lies in the collective, guided decision-making supported by leadership that favors exploration, and that is willing to trust a sensemaking process to create a map of the unfolding situation where one does not exist. This calls for adaptive crisis leadership.

"Adaptive" crisis leadership: being an unconquerable leader

In 1998, Ronald Heifetz introduced the concept of "adaptive leadership" in his book *Leadership Without Easy Answers*, based on his work with Marty Linsky and others at Harvard University. Heifetz and his colleagues realized – like many others – that singular, top-down leadership had become outdated and increasingly impractical in the then new business environment of the 1990s. It was apparent that more than ever, no single person could solve the problems confronted by a business in that new world.

To be clear, Heifetz was not writing about crisis leadership. Though the ideas he outlined have relevance for today's managers – there is actually a great deal that can be learned by a modern crisis management thinker, especially as it relates to crisis leadership.

Adaptive leadership in plain terms is defined as "the practice of mobilizing people to tackle tough problems and thrive." In a basic sense, the adaptive leadership practice sees problems in two categories. There are those which can be solved through the application of protocols, SOPs, procedures, rules, regulations, and so on. Any problems for which a manual or repeatable process can be applied – where cause and effect are reasonably known quantities – are considered "technical problems." Those problems that cannot be addressed through these methods are considered "adaptive," and were the focus of his work.

For Heifetz, these problems required solutions that were dynamic, social, and people-focused where the ability of people to connect, communicate, and innovate would win the day. The theory is that this approach could result in better business outcomes than could otherwise be realized. In fact, the researchers even favored intentionally bringing about "disequilibrium" in systems that required improvement as a way to provoke meaningful innovation and drive adaptive change. With a productive range, participants in a system could tolerate just enough distress to bring about learning and change adaptively.

In an unfolding crisis situation the disequilibrium is already present – the natural outcome of the forces of uncertainty and knowability acting on the organization and its response. The principles of adaptive leadership can then be very informative in calibrating the right leadership response in the context of the cultural aspirations outlined so far in the book. These include:

- Maintaining empathy: As a leader, the ability to intelligently perceive one's own emotional state as well as that of others is key to handling relationships. This is also central to managing stakeholders – especially those who don't feel a responsibility to be aware of their own emotional states. Well-developed emotional intelligence and empathy will enable leaders to see the people behind the issues and guide them to the right component of the solution as it emerges. This is part of resourcing for sensemaking.

- Transparency and openness: The fact that a crisis is emerging or happening cannot be closely held if an effective full-scale response is needed. Openness about what is happening, the fact that it will require a temporarily new set of responses and expectations, and a new set of goals and objectives is fundamental. For leaders this takes guts. As this text has pointed out already, living companies do well by doing right. It falls to the leaders to put this in context and take a position that the organization will be just in its response: to its people, its customers, owners, management, and the community at large. Purpose before profit will guide the decision-making and leadership values in the right direction in an adaptive setting.

- Acknowledging the learning in progress: To make everyone the problem owner, and the leader in a crisis can succeed by acknowledging some solutions will work, some will not. There should be no fear in trying new tactics based on feedback from the environment itself. The response can be led by probing, sensing, and analyzing to uncover the cause-effect unknowns. Part of the trade-off here is the risk of repeated failure or fear of it. This takes leadership with the character to admit when approaches are not fit for purpose and the willingness to change and move on quickly – in other words, to adapt.

- The Learning Process or Win-Win Problem Solving: The fourth element of adaptive leadership refers to looking for opportunities where all parties can win and raise the level of competition in a business environment for everyone. However, in the crisis context, this needs to be understood differently. Clearly, there is no benefit to raising the level of competition over the crisis.
  - Rather, this can be seen as first recognizing that the outcome of any crisis response will be both success and failure, always. There will always be wins and losses. For crisis teams this is the planning as learning model, and the crisis leader can make this part of the response – especially where experiments in the response are leading to interim failures.
  - Secondly, in a large complex organization – or in a response impacting many organizations and industries – sharing the learnings in

progress and benchmarking can be critical to gaining perspective. Crisis leaders should encourage this learning process; and such interactions should be established already as a matter of blue-sky readiness planning to the extent practical. But it is also important for the crisis leader not to simply follow the herd based on benchmarking findings. Leadership should reflect the truth of the organization's context and be true to itself above all. This may mean deviating from peer organizations if what they are doing is not consistent with an organization's own values or objectives. If that is the case, however, it can still be helpful to know. Understanding how one's own organization's response contrasts with those of a peer group is useful intelligence for decision-making processes.

These elements of adaptive crisis response suggest that leadership in the crisis context is especially effective when it is properly a social process. The effect of individuals working as a team to achieve an outcome far greater than they could have achieved on their own – against the backdrop of the unexpected or unimaginable – is a compelling idea.

The case has been made that the early recognition of a triggering event leads to better initial objectives. This leads to higher quality decision making – usually in an iterative process as the unstable situation evolves – and ultimately results in better outcomes.

The common way of imagining "leadership" is the presence of a leader, a set of followers, and a shared goal they want to achieve.

For example, there could be an Incident Commander, a set of first responders, and a burning fire they need to safely put out. In this case the focus of leadership is the establishment of the goal, the mapping of known resources to tasks, and transacting assignments.

Focus on outcomes of leadership: direction, alignment, and commitment

However, in a highly unstable and complex crisis the response might not be so simple. This is especially true in the case of business process failure or significant operational loss inside a business. The problems themselves can be just as difficult to recognize or understand as the tools and solutions needed to fix them. Even the choice of a "leader" to "command the incident" may not be immediately obvious. Once that person or people are identified it can be challenging to proceed, as already discussed.

The common examples above draw from a concept of leadership that emphasizes the individual characteristics of leaders and how they influence their followers. Without question, these are important considerations for crisis leadership. But they are also not the only features of leadership. There are other outcomes of leadership that also matter, especially in conditions of complexity and uncertainty – and where leadership needs to become as much a bottom-up process as a top-down one. These outcomes are *direction, alignment, and commitment*.[2]

In crisis –like in a competitive commercial environment – order and stability can emerge from the interaction of the various stakeholders and players. The things that prompt action in a setting like this, catalysts, can be people, ideas, behaviors, etc. Guiding the movement toward order and stability means crisis leaders need to focus on establishing a direction, some collective movement toward it, and willingness on the part of the stakeholders to proceed.

In this context, "direction" can be thought of as a consensus or agreement about the work that needs to be done, i.e. initial objectives, mission, etc. This means more than simply, "put the fire out." It means putting the immediate goals in the context of the larger organization's existing mission – and assigning the value of doing so. The challenge for the crisis leader is to recognize that direction is not uniform or limited – it can change and may need to be continuously revised or transformed. The key is that the direction does not have to be imposed by the leader. It is an outcome of the process of leadership taking place among the various stakeholders – with a figure or small team who visibly communicates it.

The notion of alignment as an outcome of crisis leadership means that the organization and coordination of knowledge and work occur in such a way that the response moves collectively toward the "direction." The alignment can happen through existing processes and formal controls – or through informal, improvised patterns. The key is coherence across the work of individual teams or groups in the organization responding to the situation. Not consistency or uniformity. But coherence – a common set of guardrails which align to the overall direction meaningfully while at the same time not prescribing action at the hyperlocal level. The simplest example might be, that a site in a multi-site company must ensure that it can adhere to local laws and regulations while also following the broader organization's direction. Where a contradiction between the two exists, the local team may be able to coordinate a solution that meets with local laws while also following the direction, or if it cannot it escalates the matter to the organization and defers to local rules.

The third outcome of crisis leadership in this model is commitment, or mutual commitment. This refers to the willingness of individual team members to align their own efforts to the collective benefit. This can be as obvious as giving up one's nights and weekends to the immediate response effort – sacrificing one's own interest for the greater cause. As an outcome of leadership this is a key challenge for leadership during long-duration responses, especially when a smaller population of stakeholders is depended upon for an extended period. Once the all-hands-on-deck phase is over, maintaining commitment becomes more difficult.

To briefly summarize, in responses with strong direction everyone has a shared understanding of what group success looks like. Where alignment is strong, the team can coordinate across roles, tasks, expertise, functions, and geography. Lastly, where commitment is high the team feels responsible for the success of the group, for one another's well-being, and they know that others feel the same. There is a level of trust that the group will see the crisis through.

Where adaptive crisis leadership can be implemented, these are outcomes of good leadership.

The next level: unboss the response?

There is another idea that diverges even further from the traditional concepts of leadership in business. In 2012, Lars Kolind and Jacob Botter published their work, Unboss, which argues that modern management practices are out of date and in need of a revolutionary change. Many of the ideas in their work have application to the problems confronting crisis leadership as a concept today.

For example, Unboss tackles head-on the culture of typical bureaucracy focused on reporting lines, processes, and traditional planning. The trade-off for an organization in terms of the control, order, and accountability this provides, is offset by the stifling of any attribute required to be agile or responsive to change. Unboss looks to take away the idea that bosses should be in control of subordinates in favor of collaboration among employees in an organization that views its borders more broadly to include its customers, suppliers, users, members, and the community at large in collaboration.

The solution – as in De Geus' work – is to place purpose before profit; break down silos; and reward creativity, partnership, and innovation.

Clearly these approaches won't work for every organization – and even when they do, they need to be adopted as part of a holistic culture that makes sense for the company. But there are some aspects of Unboss that have real potential for improving crisis management outcomes, especially as it relates to leadership.

The notion in Unboss that may be the most accessible is that leadership should not be defined by a role or a title. Instead, the Unbossed leader is a servant to the team; a person who is motivated by purpose, inclusive and capable of inspiring others, and focused on working across boundaries to further collaboration. In Kolind and Botter's formulation, this means anyone can be an Unboss – not just those in positions of authority or power. In the context of crisis management leadership, this can often be the case.

These are the things that "unbossed crisis leaders" do to bring out the best in others – when it matters most:

- Be clear on purpose. Know what matters most to the people involved. From there, align toward the outcomes – direction, alignment, and commitment.
- Remove obstacles. The adaptive crisis leader's role is to clear a path for the team to build experiments, check them, and direct sensemaking. As challenges to the process emerge, the leader's job is to get the obstacles out of the way so the team can stay focused.
- Empower and support others. Leadership in crisis depends on the ability of people on the edges of the organization – where the solutions and signals that matter most may be – to speak up comfortably. Leaders have a responsibility to foster the conditions where that can occur.
- Create clarity and accountability. Especially when conditions are changing quickly and information is incomplete or unknowable, the leader has a responsibility to ensure that stakeholders are making clear and understandable requests of one another and that requests are responded to in a timely and meaningful way.

- Collaboration. Leaders have the ability to see beyond immediate organizational borders and into other lanes. It is a leader's responsibility to ensure that collaboration across the organization is taking place – and that in a crisis nothing is being missed at core operational levels that could be integral to the response.

In settings where leaders embrace and role model these kinds of unbossed qualities, a team can experience a greater sense of safety with taking appropriate risks, or even freedom to do so. High performance crisis teams begin to take on the qualities of the good adaptive crisis leader. Admittedly, "unboss" is a term which can be problematic or at the very least eyebrow raising. It is not for everyone or every organization. Especially in the context of a high-stakes crisis response. Clearly the time to introduce these concepts is not in the initial response phase of a looming crisis, but rather as part of the overall blue-sky planning and program readiness. But that doesn't mean there isn't tremendous value in some of these ideas that can be incorporated into any crisis response – in part even, if not as a whole. One of the most important and challenging of these for crisis leaders is collaboration.

The traditional approach is to think of collaboration as a value to cultivate rather than a skill that can be taught. The problem is, in a crisis context many of the same obstacles that exist to collaboration normally are amplified. And newer problems can emerge – such as self-deployment or misalignment.

The answer for leaders is to focus on establishing and following guiding principles, then relax steering and control to the extent practical. If this can be achieved, then the team is on its way to "unbossing" the response.

The right kind of crisis leader

What makes a good crisis leader? What makes an individual effective in a crisis leadership role?

A smart person once said, "You meet a different version of yourself during a crisis." Most crisis management professionals know this and are familiar with the version of themselves they meet in those situations.

There is a persistent myth that the crisis leader is supremely self-assured, practically omniscient, in possession of a detailed playbook with checklists for every eventuality, and fully tireless. The reality could probably be further from the truth. Crisis leaders are just people. Most often they are people who didn't expect to be responding to a crisis that particular day, but now find themselves with accountability for an outcome beyond their control.

It is also true that not everyone is suited to working in, let alone taking the responsibility for leadership, in exceedingly stressful situations. Plain and simple, like anything else, some people are just better at it than others. Most business school courses and training prepare leaders to manage in "ordered domains" (i.e. the clear and complicated Cynefin contexts); but many practical business problems and nearly all crises exist in "unordered domains," especially the "complex" Cynefin context. Where protocols and procedures are of no use, and the link between cause and effect is not known, good leaders often depend on intuition, charisma, and personal characteristics. These are, of course, tremendously valuable, but often innate characteristics.

The good news is that through training and experience crisis leadership can be learned. There are frameworks that can help leaders navigate complexity and bring about calm, clarity, and focus – while also instilling these qualities in the team around them.

Crisis management theory and traditional planning do not spend a lot of time focused on how to get the right person in command. In most cases, this is a part of the job description for leaders at an organization during the normal course of business. Preparation for leadership during times of crisis is not necessarily a focus of attention. There is a role, therefore, for a well-functioning crisis team to provide support to a leader who hasn't experienced crisis before. By being guardians of the process, helping map the steps as they are taken, and anticipating what lies ahead, the crisis team can help leaders lead from behind the scenes.

In practical terms, the right kind of crisis leader should be capable of the following:

- Framing: The right kind of crisis leader can define what is happening in terms beyond the apparent issue. They have the ability to place the immediate situation, its implications, and the presence of the unknown into context and to communicate that context in a way that people can connect with.
- Forecasting and Anticipation: Without falling into panic, the right crisis leader can see the implications for various stakeholders and anticipate their impacts to guide the response.

- Critical Thinking: This is a basic expectation of any leader, but it is critical that the ability to assess divergent views on core assets not be lost as a result of the situation.
- Own the Guiding Principles: The ability to know the organization's values well enough to know where they matter, and where they can or cannot be compromised, is key to leading an effective response.
- Stakeholder Management: The ability to truly know stakeholders and their positions, and have the ability to negotiate with them on response dilemmas is a core function of an effective crisis leader.

What crisis leadership does

The things that a leader has to do in crisis (as well as in the service of an organization's readiness) in some ways resemble normal operating conditions, with the volume turned all the way up. In other ways, the things that leaders are called upon to do in responding to crisis are completely unique. This section is an exploration of the crisis leadership in action.

What should a crisis leader do? What tools and models are available for understanding crisis leadership? There is a great deal of valuable information and research available on the topic of crisis leadership. For the purposes of this book, the focus is on those leadership activities that best enable an organization to respond as a whole system – including at the edges – with a particular emphasis on the practical aspects. Some of these are strategic, longer-term, bigger picture activities; and some of these are the applied day-to-day activities that a leader is called upon to own.

Bear in mind that even when taking an approach like the one encouraged here, with loosened central control and a principles and values-based style, there can remain a role to play for the leader that may look more traditional. Some of that is discussed here. Ultimately, however, crisis leadership is to an extent a function of the individual leader's character. The crisis leader can wear the traditional role of a commanding presence while briefing the Board of Directors (if that suits the circumstances), while also acting as a servant leader and even creating an unbossed environment for the responding teams. In other words, the appearance of these two roles need not be mutually exclusive.

From a strategic point of view, the crisis leader should consider four things: 1) coalescing the team with a "time-out" in order to 2) frame up the situation and anticipate stakeholder concerns, then 3) preparing some of those stakeholders proactively, and 4) establishing the story of the crisis in context using the cynefin model or similar framework.

A strategic toolkit for the unconquerable crisis leader

- **Call a time out**

  By the time a crisis leader is in place, much of the initial baseline assessment described previously in this book is probably complete or underway.

  Some level of escalation has taken place and as part of it an assessment of the situation is available. Some notifications have already been made, but perhaps not all. Basic objectives – or the three initial ones (life safety, incident stability, and property/environmental protection) – are coming together.

  The leader needs to begin the process of framing the situation from a strategic perspective in order to guide the coalescing team around a direction, form alignment, and hopefully establish commitment.

  These initial parts and pieces need to be reviewed so that a map of the next steps can come together. This needs to be done in an intentional, deliberate manner – not in the heat of the opening salvos of whatever is happening. And it is worth pointing out that teamwork can be hard in conditions of stress and extreme complexity. To manage through this, the first step a leader can take is to call a "Time Out."

  This is a literal stop in the action. Pencils, laptops, phones, etc. down. Eyes up. If even virtually. The conversation stops and all attention should be on the leadership. In confrontation with a fundamentally complex, unknown or emerging risk a lot begins to happen all at once. Individual players and subunits begin to prioritize their own actions and resource needs and seek a solution. In some cases, this urgent focus can lead to one of the most common and dangerous team dynamics: silent disengagement. Where focused, specialized professionals begin to delve into their domains in search of answers, and a "stay in your lane" or "that's not my job" mentality can emerge. It may sound obvious, but one of the most effective guards against this is to simply have the team stop and talk through the situation together. This has become common practice among medical practitioners before a surgery, with military units before an operation, with construction and repair reams before a task. In any setting where there is a cross functional team that doesn't commonly interact, but who shares a common task, the time-out meeting can be a saving grace. And it doesn't have to be complicated.

The objective of the time-out meeting is to frame the situation and establish the next steps which are the beginnings of answers to the questions: *"What needs to be done?,"* and *"Who's doing what?"*

Preparing for and Leading the Time Out Meeting

Prior to calling a time out – if at all practical – it is helpful to give the relevant stakeholders a heads up and ask that they be prepared to speak to their areas in a few minutes for one- or two bullet points each. This allows the team members and stakeholders a brief moment to collect themselves and prepare.

The key points in the meeting should be to clarify why the situation has escalated.

1. Has the team followed an escalation protocol?
2. If so, what triggered the escalation?
3. Is there agreement as to nature of the triggering event? Does the team understand what is known about what occurred?
4. Is it clear what is not yet known?
5. Who has been notified and who still needs to be notified?

The Outcome of the time-out

The crisis leader will take the opportunity in the time-out to quickly clarify what is happening, remove any immediate obstacles, and set the tone for the next phase of the response. It can be helpful to repeat back a summary of the incident status to confirm it is understood.

The expectations can be made clear that the team will guide and lead decision making; that all decisions will be iterative; that uncertainty and knowability are working against them; but that the organization's values will not be compromised.

For the crisis leader there are two concurrent paths to follow: service to the responding team or teams; and duty to the organization's ownership or senior-most leadership. The product of these two paths is the framing that the leader creates around the situation.

- As it relates to the responding team, this means the crisis leader has a role in reviewing – or even challenging – the team's initial objectives, identifying the immediate obstacles to progress, assigning resources and teams to follow up on them, and developing an action/resource tracking capability (more on this to follow).

- With regard to the organization's senior leadership or ownership, the crisis leader has a duty to provide updates, guidance, respond to inquiries and support the fiduciary duty of organizational leadership. To achieve this the leader must be able to frame the situation.

- **Frame the situation: focus on effects, anticipate stakeholder concerns**

  The crisis leader more than anyone else has a duty to maintain a current, accurate, and balanced view of what is happening. What is the story being told, and where are we in it?

  This should be derived directly from the operational response and crisis team's inputs. It can also be informed by the leader's individual perspective. To this extent, that person's ability to see the unfolding crisis as a "story" and deploy the storytelling, sensemaking tools in establishing context around the circumstances can be of great value. There are times when reporting the facts alone without conjecture is necessary; there are also times when building a narrative around what is happening is important. It can fall to the leader to know what needs to be said and how it should be said to a given stakeholder.

  The key is to build context – frame. This requires the ability to define the crisis beyond just the obvious or known facts. The frame for the situation is defined by what key assets are in peril or at risk. Thinking back to preparing for effects vs causes, there are basically three: the unexpected unavailability of people, places and things.

  1. Staff,
  2. Facilities, and
  3. Critical Resources.

By starting with these effects, the leader can narrow the discussion with stakeholders and the universe of possible questions. Most of the questions – in the early stages – will not be immediately answerable anyway. The best approach is to take the effects, analyze them one step further and map them to stakeholders. The intent is to anticipate the potential stakeholder interests and be in a position to respond.

This can be done quickly as part of a "clean container" exercise in the early moments. This rapid analysis can form the basis for a set of talking points that the crisis team can use for reference.

Table 6.1 is an example – not all inclusive, but just a sample for consideration.

Table 6.1 Example of a clean container, mapping effects to assets and stakeholder impact

Effects (unexpected unavailability)	Relevant assets	Anticipated stakeholders/impacts
People	Staff Customers	Employees, their families Customers/Visitors Community Members Critical contractors Management Board of Directors
Places	Facilities	Critical operations Physical and Intellectual property
Things	Critical Resources	Critical vendors Product and service safety; delivery Brand, reputation, and trust Shareholder value

From this very rudimentary example, what should become apparent is that a cascade from effects, to impacts on relevant assets to anticipated stakeholder issues can be done reasonably quickly and offer a baseline for clarifying the basic elements of some talking points to frame the incident early on.

For example, using the "frame" above, a leader could quickly identify what they know and what they don't know – and what they can say to a CEO, for instance.

Example of Talking Points based on the Frame:

1. *"The ongoing incident began at 8am local time, is still in progress and is being assessed by the team."*

   This point establishes a temporal baseline (something just happened) and sets the expectation that information is still incomplete, but that answers will be forthcoming and a team is in place.

2. *"There are staff and customers at the impacted site. Ten are confirmed safe. We are making contact with the rest using our notification tool, but we cannot estimate when they will all be accounted for. We will report an update within the next hour."*

   Establish the status of the life safety objective first, always. And report only what is confirmed. Clarify when the next update on this objective will be available and commit to providing it, even if no information becomes available.

3. *"The location hosts several critical operations. These functions are suspended at present and we anticipate a customer impact. Our team is working with local operations to clarify downtime."*

   Clarify the context around what the incident means for the business' operations to the extent it can be known, especially if there are critical customers or business operations potentially at stake.

4. *"Our critical vendors were also impacted by this incident and will not be available to immediately assist us."*

   Identify any resource constraints or obstacles that can be known up-front. Use this to set expectations that this may impact recovery timelines, to confirm that the usual processes will not be possible, and that as a consequence the stakeholder may either have to revise their expectations or become part of the solution.

5. The final point in the frame should consist of any request for a decision or action on the part of the stakeholder; and a firm commitment on when the next update will occur. Meeting that commitment is a major opportunity for the crisis leader to build trust with stakeholders. Even if there is no meaningful update, providing a quick note to say just that will earn trust for the team.

- **Focus on what is next: anticipate the next operational period**

  The crisis leader needs to serve the team by seeking to stay as far ahead of the situation as possible. The focus should be not so much on what is occurring now, but what needs to occur next. "Next" being the coming 12 hour shift, 24 hour day, or other meaningful increment: the operational period.

That requires providing guidance to help the team organize their activities and decision-making around some of the following:

o   What needs to start happening,
o   What needs to stop,
o   What must continue
o   And who is going to do it? (more on this later)

These questions should be linked to a loose time frame – in answer to the question "when" for each. This can be either on an immediate basis, within minutes, hours, days or beyond.

While directing this process, the crisis leader has the opportunity both to role model and observe among the team the kinds of behaviors that will drive better outcomes.

a. Caring and compassion – the well-being of people comes first.
b. The assumption of positive intent. Start from the position that people are doing their best to help in trying circumstances. Not everyone responds to extraordinary stress well, and people respond in all sorts of ways.
c. All stakeholders' needs will be addressed in a timely manner. No matter how small or seemingly irrelevant or low priority. The team as a whole will depend upon the organization it serves to trust it – this is critical to its success. Earning and safeguarding the trust of stakeholders should not be underestimated even in the earliest stages.
d. All decisions and actions will be guided by honesty, ethics, and the law. This cannot be compromised.
e. Maintain open, visible, and available communication with teams and stakeholders at any time. Make use of the time-out regularly as conditions demand.

•   **Addressing boards of directors (as well as owners or senior-most leadership) – get proactive**

An often overlooked, but critically important, function for crisis leaders involves addressing the stakeholders at the uppermost levels of an organization. While this book focuses most on the edges of the organization, and bringing in signals and expertise from across all levels – the fact remains that in a crisis situation, the Board, Ownership, and senior leaders are key stakeholders.

Handling these stakeholders is worthy of its own discussion. First, it should be said that through much experience if this category of stakeholder is not addressed, they can intervene in a response in ways that can be disruptive or counterproductive. The reasons for this vary, and they are not all derived from bad intentions. These leaders have unique and very hi-stakes concerns, duties, and responsibilities that must be met when crisis conditions occur. For this reason, it can be helpful for the crisis team to be proactive in addressing them. A crisis leader himself may be called upon to address senior leadership, or they may be asked to assist or coach an internal stakeholder (like a Vice President or CEO) to speak about the crisis response.

It is also worth noting that because of the frequency and severity of crisis situations globally, Boards of Directors and major corporations are increasingly being asked or coached to assess their company's crisis response capabilities. Part of this is driven by the types of disaster that are occurring. PWC's 2019 *Global Crisis Survey* found that among 2,000 global companies, nearly all had experienced one or more incidents that they would describe as a "crisis" in the preceding five years. The most common types of incidents they experienced included the expected traditional, kinetic situations (such as terrorist attacks, security incidents, workplace violence) and natural disasters – situations for which most large organizations have evolved some level of readiness. Interestingly, the companies surveyed also reported that none of these types rose to the top five on the list of incident types. The most common "crises" were actually operational failures, technological failures, reputational issues, and financial liquidity issues. These are incident types that reflect much greater complexity for response teams, lend themselves much less to preplanned responses, and depend to a high degree on an integrated response.

In 2021, PWC and the Conference Board conducted a survey entitled, "Board Effectiveness: A survey of the C-suite",[3] intended to gauge perception of 556 senior executives at US public companies in over a dozen industries about their own boards of directors. This survey found that only 37% of senior executives believed that their boards of directors crisis expertise was "good" or "excellent." More than half of respondents believed their boards understood their own company's crisis plans "very well" or "somewhat well." Across the ten areas where this survey assessed director's knowledge, they were perceived as performing the lowest in the area of crisis readiness.

Company executives have commonly cited crisis management as a vulnerability that was exposed at their companies as a result of COVID-19. During a time when every company was facing the crisis, plans and responses were in the limelight and often found to be lacking – especially in terms of their deployment and effectiveness at the senior-most levels.

This has significant strategic implications for a crisis leader.

○ First, from a blue sky perspective, it means that boards and senior leaders are more likely to proactively seek out participation in planning and exercising than in the past, perhaps. It is likely that they have been made newly aware or concerned with their duties and responsibilities in this area. This creates the opportunity for the crisis team (again, on a blue sky basis) to provide tremendous value to the organization by giving senior leaders a proper grounding in a holistic crisis response like the one recommended here.

○ Second, it suggests that when a crisis hits, the board or senior leaders – who's primary day to day role is not in crisis response – may be at varying levels of readiness or willingness to respond.

Among other things, Boards are responsible for overseeing the work of management in public companies. They ensure that the organization has the proper planning and strategy in place to meet its commercial objectives over the short and long terms. Boards are central to corporate governance and have duties to all stakeholders in that regard – including external partners, shareholders, investors, and the public. Because of this broad mandate, crisis readiness is not usually central to their priorities when things are going well.

Nevertheless, they are responsible for company stewardship and oversight – to include ensuring proactive prevention against known risks, promoting and safeguarding company reputation, and even explicit crisis planning.

As a crisis leader responding to an ongoing incident, it can be helpful to know how to handle these stakeholders. To brief a board directly, or to support an executive in briefing them, it is worthwhile to consider the following messages and prepare along these lines in providing assurance to a board and senior leaders.

- o   Respect the likelihood that board directors may be predisposed to address the crisis directly, and to attempt to be part of the solution. Unless specified in a crisis plan, it is worth cautioning against direct involvement as any such action is likely to be scrutinized and possibly criticized in any related media reporting or subsequent investigation or litigation.
  - • Where possible the crisis plan should be constructed in such a way, or a separate plan generated for Board Members, which provides them with a set of role expectations and rules of engagement. This can include seeking to minimize the burden on the responding crisis team itself.
- o   The Board and Senior Leaders offer a unique perspective, often reflecting external factors that may not have occurred to the response team who are immersed in the immediate and day-to-day matters. Be prepared to ask and be asked a variety of questions related to the response.
  - • This may include a check against the reliability of known information and potential access to additional sources to verify unknown information.
  - • Have adequate resources been assigned to support the response team, over and above assumptions? What obstacles remain or are impassable?
  - • Is decision making and balance needed around strategic communication matters, potential liability, and the assumption of responsibility if and when appropriate?
  - • Can the Board offer assurance to the team that their direction is sound, consistent with the organization's stated mission and culture, and lending support to the response as a whole?
- o   Leave the discussion with a commitment to follow up. If the Board hasn't already engaged in blue sky planning, they may welcome the opportunity to do so in the future when the present matter is concluded. For that discussion, give consideration to the following:

- Have the Board evaluate the crisis readiness approach, and the planning assumptions in it?
- Seek clarity around the level of crisis that would threaten the viability of the organization, and thus would require Board involvement.
- Consider alignment between the crisis management program and the enterprise risk management process.
- Construct a stakeholder list and communications plan that ensures the CEO/President and senior most leaders are not over-loaded in a crisis – but have the space and ability to focus on strategic commercial priorities,
- Identify who will, how, and when to communicate with the investor community – obtain alignment on this in advance.
- Commit to an annual exercise and readiness review.

The board of directors and senior executive class are a unique category of stakeholder, not unlike elected officials in the public sector context. For this reason, it is important to give consideration to their needs and responsibilities. For the crisis leader, this falls under the category of service to the organization. The crisis team can have a distinct role in helping these leaders to lead, while at the same time accepting their input and guidance.

- **Cynefin for crisis leaders: from chaos to complexity**
  So much about leadership has to do with individual characteristics, soft skills, charisma, the ability to motivate others, gain trust and use influence and persuasion. Some of this can be learned, and some of it is innate. The model introduced earlier in this book, the Cynefin Framework, is a tool that is worth consideration by those who find themselves in a leadership position in crisis.

  Earlier, the Cynefin Framework was shown as a way of managing initial complexity. But it also has significant value for leaders in terms of orienting circumstances to strategy and placing an emerging situation into some form of context (especially where none may seem present).

  Essentially, if leaders can *sense* which of the Cynefin contexts they are in, they can potentially guide better decisions while also avoiding potential pitfalls.

In the Clear Context, patterns repeat, cause and effect can be understood plainly, and variables are known. In this setting, line workers and frontline operations have a complete grasp of matters and should be trusted to respond accordingly. This is considered the realm of procedure. For the person in the leadership position there is no need to micromanage this situation. Basic delegation, direct communication and best practices should be the rule. For the crisis team, this is the context where frontline operations have enormously valuable intuition, or an ability to sense before others where anomalies may emerge that could lead into other contexts. The crisis leader's role here is not really relevant, because there should be no crisis at this stage. Instead, culture should enable reporting of anomalies, and assumptions about best practices should be periodically and gently challenged.

Moving to the Complicated Context, good practices – rather than best practices – take priority. Cause and effect patterns are knowable, but not immediately apparent to everyone because they require some level of expert analysis or diagnosis. In this realm, fact based management still rules. Most significantly, for the crisis leader, there can be more than one right answer. The leader's role here should include guiding the sense-analyze-respond discussion where proper expert opinion is collected and conflicting advice is considered. The pitfall in this realm – especially for crisis leaders – is failing to recognize that multiple solutions can result in nearly equal outcomes. Insisting on one solution over others can be destabilizing to the team.

The Complex Context is the realm of "unknown unknowns" and is where most crisis responses will occur. This context is characterized by a lack of correlation between cause and effect; or patterns of cause and effect that can only be understood in the aftermath. There can be no right answers – only emergent patterns that result from the interaction of different ideas, observations, and innovative approaches. This is the most challenging area for the crisis leader. The temptation will be strong to lean into command-control style approaches and demand defined outcomes (failing to realize that they cannot exist). Overcontrolling a situation like this will doom it to failure. Added to these stressors, the best possible path out of a complex situation is failure through experiment which paradoxically can be the hardest to tolerate in such conditions. The leader's role is to focus on creating the environment where the necessary interaction and experimentation can occur, while fending off the fear of consequences and pressure from outside stakeholders. Monitoring for and pulling out emergent patterns from the interaction of the teams should be the focus.

It can also be very helpful for the crisis leader to recognize that team members and various stakeholders will commonly reflect biases from the context they most often inhabit. In other words, those who work in Clear contexts (such as production, engineering, or linear processes) will be inclined to view problems as failure of process.

On the other hand, "experts" who mostly work in the world of Complicated contexts (medicine, labs, technology) where experimentation and analysis go hand in hand will be inclined to perceive the cause of a problem as a failure of resource allocation or proper analysis.

Complexity workers usually do well in crisis settings and have a comfort with bringing together diverse players in pursuit of a solution.

Finally, the Chaotic Context. These circumstances are impossibly turbulent with no clear solution, no cause/effect relationship, high tension and are resistant to calm reasoning or fact based management. Quite simply, these conditions demand action directed at pushing circumstances into another domain – Complex, Complicated, or Clear.

What is the crisis leader to do with this model?

○ Assume Complexity.

  If there is a "crisis situation" which calls for leadership, by definition is not "Clear" in the Cynefin sense of the word. Assuming no immediate action is needed (i.e. Chaos), then start from the position that the circumstances are Complex, anticipate a Probe-Sense-Respond approach will be needed and get ready for pattern-based (rather than fact based) leadership.

○ Open Communication

  Identify a team, gather them, call a Time-Out and set the tone for an ongoing, iterative discussion aimed at some set of initial objectives.

○ Establish Expectations

  Guide the team in understanding that the situation is Complex (in the Cynefin sense) and not clear or chaotic. Action must be taken, but there is time to arrive at a solution. There may be more than one viable answer. The cause/effect relationships may not be knowable. This team will need to work together to identify the patterns that will solve the problem.

o   There is no Cause and Effect. Get the Probe and Sense Started.
    Unleash the team and experts to begin attracting signals and phenomenon with potential for solutions. Encourage dissent and diversity of thought, but monitor for the emergence of meaningful patterns. When patterns develop, help the team focus attention by anchoring back to the primary objectives. The leader needs to walk the line between encouraging experimental thought and keeping the team out of the weeds of unfruitful or irrelevant avenues for exploration.

Learning to let go without losing command: principled decisions and ethics in crisis leadership

In an earlier chapter, this book looked at how Helmuth von Moltke and other military leaders learned to gain an advantage by loosening control. By permitting "subordinate" leaders in the complex military organization to act on initiative in response to circumstances, commanders witnessed far better outcomes than by direct orders alone.

There is a persuasive argument that achieving this style of looser command and control is actually much easier in military contexts than in commercial enterprises, for example. It is also true that commercial enterprises have begun to recognize the value of these approaches and now work hard to integrate them into their cultures, to varying levels of effectiveness. Like so many things in today's environment, it is easier said than done. There is a difference between having a corporate culture that speaks to agility and resilience, and truly giving people the ability to be agile and resilient. Every organization and company has stated mission and objectives – those things that tell people what to do; and they all have SOPs and rules and guidelines that tell employees how to do it. But far fewer companies have been successful in creating a singular, contextualized set of principles or ethics that give individuals the tools to make decisions across the organization.

Without this piece – principles or ethics – it is difficult for managers and leaders to "unboss" without losing control. It is much easier for managers to fall back into direct oversight and supervision, reliance on prescriptive rules and dependence on permission instead of the team's intuition and initiative.

When the unexpected happens, crisis teams and their leaders are presented with an opportunity. Much of the practice of crisis management has to do with bucking existing systems and bureaucracy in the service of the immediate response goals. To achieve this, crisis teams work and think differently, including in the ways presented in this book. That also creates an opportunity for the crisis leader to introduce – even temporarily – a culture for the crisis team around the response that favors initiative and deliberate independent action (within reason) that may go a little further than what the previous culture considered normal.

By no means is this a recommendation for self-deployment and an anything goes style response

This is a proposal that crisis leaders take the opportunity to instill a set of basic guiding principles for the response team. Principles serve to allow that team to make good, independent decisions without weighing down the response organization with requests for approval. Principles give subteams the latitude to respond to quickly changing circumstances in ways that makes sense. They are the tools the team members use to put the idea into action that "For right now, *you are trusted to know what the right thing to do is. And you are expected to do it.*"

This is the way in which the crisis leader can become "Unconquerable." Recognizing the context, creating the right conditions for the team to function as described above, and loosening control just enough. It should become apparent that the elements of crisis management described so far have a compounding effect to this point. Early recognition enabled by good input from the edges of the organization; a rapid responsible escalation; leading to sound initial objectives. With these boxes checked, the leader and the team – acting together – are in a position to lead good principle based decisions.

As a practical matter, these activities can be integrated into a few steps:

- First, be very clear on the "why" of what is happening. Create alignment and direction around initial objectives.

- Next, be upfront about the risks. Acknowledge that the present circumstances are unexpected or unprecedented and will require similarly unplanned responses (possibly). Elicit feedback on the risks that entails, but encourage smart risk taking.
- Seek out and value alternative courses of action and hypotheses. Identify options without feeling the need to fully and immediately vet and analyze them (initially). Prioritize the most suitable.
- Lastly, reach a decision. Again, not based on what all of the possible available information says; but rather a decision derived from the assessment of relevant experts based on the need for action.

The circumstances in a crisis call for a certain degree of boldness. This can be achieved without being impulsive or authoritarian as long as the leader, and consequently the team, act with clear intent, link their work to the broader objectives, value diverse perspectives, and sincerely work to make a positive difference.

Even under the harshest of circumstances this can be achieved, and never is it more important to lead from this perspective than when things are potentially at their worst. For an individual leader this won't be possible every moment of every response. But it is a worthy aspiration, especially if these behaviors become a pattern that can be modeled by the team and thereby take on a positive life of their own.

Putting principles and ethics into action – be bold, but not reckless

Consider the examples of a few well recognized brands who have established a cultural identity for themselves around these ideas. While not specific to their "crisis management" programs per se, these examples offer a glimpse of what principles or ethics in action can look like and may serve as inspiration for the crisis leader in search of a model.

Wikipedia, operated by the not-for-profit Wikimedia Foundation, has a detailed set of community policies and guidelines which lay out the guardrails for Wikipedia as "…a self-governing project run by its community. Its policies and guidelines are intended to reflect the consensus of the community." Contained within these documents are all the things that make

Wikipedia run and are understood by its community. They collectively are summarized as Five Pillars.

- Wikipedia is an Encyclopedia.
- Wikipedia is written from a neutral point of view.
- Wikipedia is free content that anyone can use, edit, and distribute.
- Wikipedia's editors should treat each other with respect and civility.
- Wikipedia has no firm rules.

These Five Pillars define what the organization is, what it is not, how it should work, how its editors should conduct themselves and defines authority – or the lack of firm rules. The Pillars end with the closing remark, "Be Bold, but not reckless."

Another interesting example is Visa, under the leadership of former CEO Dee Hock. One of Hock's well known opening remarks to audiences involved holding up a Visa card – his Visa card – and asking who could tell him where the company was headquartered, how it was governed or where to buy its shares. More often than not, no one would know because they had never really thought about it. And that was exactly the point. For Hock, the better an organization is, the less obvious it has to be. He created what he described as an "invisible organization," which was in part rooted in his belief that rigid command and control models in banking and finance had become irrelevant, and even destructive. Instead, what Hock created was a decentralized and highly collaborative enterprise with everything – including decision making, initiative, ownership of action – pushed as far out the edges as possible. Hock imagined a business who's product is coordination.

Consider also Red Hat's Open Organization. Describing itself as "the largest open source company in the world," Red Hat is a global enterprise technology provider. They drive their workers to "be greater than the sum of their parts" by sharing common values of Freedom, Courage, Commitment, and Accountability. These are balanced with the principles of Purpose, Passion, Community, and Opportunity to create an environment where a wide range of technical experts and managers from across many functions and disciplines can collaborate.

To the extent that a given organization has established such principles as guides to behavior, the crisis leader should take the opportunity to amplify them within the response. Or, in settings where such guides don't already exist, it is worthwhile to make them a part of the "clean container" presented by the crisis itself. There is always the possibility that some of it will stick even after the smoke clears.

Being unconquerable in leadership means becoming a "Gardener"

The knee-jerk response to crisis and the unexpected by organizations and the people that lead them is usually to collect more and better information, resources, and control. On an individual level, leaders will often feel the strong urge to gather up and seize as much control as they can – which is a very human response.

While understandable, it bears repeating that crisis situations – situations of expanding or unknown complexity – present the organization with friction. Removing the friction is key to driving out of the crisis, but paradoxically the instinct to grab control and centralize it has the opposite effect on the responding team. This can cause the team in turn to start gathering up unrelated information and serving up the chain in the form of inquiries and requests for permission to act, in the process creating burdens on the response and unnecessary time delays.

John Boyd – military strategist, organizational theorist, and the creator of the OODA Loop – observed this phenomenon a generation ago in the US military. His presentation "Organic Design for Command and Control" lays out his solution, which still holds true today, and is rooted in the "implicit nature of human beings." Boyd favored an approach that fostered independent initiative over direct command where leaders support the conditions for informed responses by the players involved, without prescribing what they must do.

More recently, a contemporary military leader encountered these challenges again in a new context and took the ideas further. When Stanley McChrystal took over leadership for the US Joint Special Operations Task Force Command in 2005 he inherited one of the most well prepared, well trained, organized and capable military organizations in the world. Yet, with access to nearly limitless resources and the best intelligence available, his teams were being meaningfully challenged and sometimes defeated on the streets of Iraq by poorly equipped, untrained, under resourced insurgents and terrorists.

The reason for this, McChrystal concluded, had nothing to do with their relative strength or access to resources and training. It had to do with US leadership and organization. Effectively, al Qaeda in Iraq at the time was resilient to McChrystal's forces because it could conduct frequent, small, high-risk operations continuously. Operations which presented high risk both to the individual attackers and to the al-Qaeda organization in Iraq itself. Whereas the Joint Special Forces Command had evolved to accomplish a few well-organized high-risk missions a year – missions which presented very high risk to the teams involved, but not to the organization as a whole.

This incongruity explained why the US forces weren't keeping pace with their adversaries and the solution, for McChrystal, lay in reducing internal friction in the US organization and increasing the frequency of their own operations.

To achieve this, there needed to be a change in the Joint Special Operations Task Force's organization. McChrystal prioritized information sharing (structuring to bring in the edges of the organization, improving intelligence flow locally, and breaking barriers to communication); he delegated decision making to the front lines rather than focusing decision making up a chain of command; and promoted the idea of the leader as the "gardener."

In other words, McChrystal saw the difficulty for a leader staying credible and legitimate when they haven't done what the people they are leading are doing. It shatters the image of the "heroic" leader – the supreme commander who can swoop in and define a path with certainty and absolute control. The alternative is a humble gardener who tends, rather than controls. A leader who listens, observes, and cultivates rather than directs and commands.

For a leader who aspires to be unconquerable in crisis this is a powerful lesson. Every stakeholder interaction, however, big or small, is meaningful and can leave a lasting impact on a person for better or worse. This effect is amplified in crisis conditions. Leaders have to lead by example, holding themselves and others accountable builds trust. Willingness to listen and learn from those at any level of the organization requires checking the ego and knowing one's own limitations. Being transparent, owning mistakes and learning from them, and accepting the growth that can come from failure will win the day.

TAKEAWAY

When crisis strikes, orient the team to the Cynefin framework: are circumstances "complex," "chaotic," or "complicated?" Recognize that the Cynefin context may help define the response – especially where a tightly controlled response will simply not work, as in the "complex" context.

Escalate information flow upward and across silos only as far and fast as needed.

Delegate decision making down as much as practical.

Reduce internal friction wherever possible: eliminate self-imposed organizational red-tape.

Prioritize communication over instruction – make sure people are talking to each other locally.

Convey the value of acting on good judgment over simply following procedure until circumstances return to a more clear state.

Crises are a time when other than normal leadership is required. "Crisis leaders" do not have to hold a title or a position (though it helps if they do as a result of good blue sky planning). Experience helps, but it need not be a prerequisite. The crisis leader is a servant leader – someone who can motivate a broad population of experts and responders, and galvanize their vision for what needs to be done into practical action.

The crisis leader helps the team bring clarity and stability to situations where there is none. They favor exploration over certainty and are willing to allow a sensemaking process work in a way that creates a map of what is really taking place.

Remember, like Wikipedia says in its Pillars, "be bold, not reckless."

Notes

1. Steven Horowitz, "Best Responders: Post-Katrina Innovation and Improvisation by WalMart and the US Coast Guard," Innovations. Spring 2009, p. 94.

2. Wildred H. Drath, et al., "Direction, alignment, commitment: Toward a more integrative ontology of leadership," Leadership Quarterly, Vol 19, Number 6, December 2008.

3. See Paul DeNicola, "Board Effectiveness: A survey of the C-suite," PWC.com; and "The Crisis Management Crisis – and how boards can overcome it," https://www.pwc.com/us/en/services/governance-insights-center/blog/crisis-management-boards.html

7

"WHAT NEEDS TO BE DONE?" – DEFINING PRIORITIES & ACTION MANAGEMENT

The preceding chapter covered some of the elements of good leadership in crisis. In this chapter the next key question is explored: "What Needs to be Done?"

This question deals with defining priorities, translating them into action, tracking those actions, conducting team briefings, and managing information and intelligence. There are many ways of achieving these things. What follows is not comprehensive, but intended to provoke the reader into thinking differently about priority setting and action management.

In essence, the answer to this question entails going from sensemaking to meaningful action. It is the bridge between the tone and direction created (in part) by the crisis leader, and the solutions and good decision-making that the team will deliver.

The case of the potted plant

In the early spring of 2020, COVID-19 had just begun to take hold in the US. Every major company in the world was managing its own internal crisis response, trying to keep their people safe and managing stakeholders.

DOI: 10.4324/9781003216803-10

The unknowns far outnumbered the knowns, and new protocols had to be established on the fly every day in every imaginable context to keep critical operations running. This was truly a complex context (in the Cynefin sense of the word).

At one global company, a US-based leadership team had convened with its crisis team to address some urgent stakeholder concerns. Several weeks into COVID-19, the team had already pivoted to remote work for all but the most critical workers. Key business processes were being managed through now extended and weary workarounds. Resources were stretched, the virus was still presenting new challenges every day, and much work remained to ensure the viability of the business.

While all of this was taking place, a particular leadership team became focused on providing for the comfort, health, and psychological well-being of their now entirely remote workers. This concern was fully consistent with the company's culture and came from a good place. However, the concern grew into a preoccupation as members of the team competed to present the most creative solution to the remote worker comfort question. A debate spiraled into a plan to send ornate potted plants to each of the thousands of workers who had been newly displaced from corporate offices to their own homes.

What began as a well-intentioned gesture appeared to take on the appearance of a fully fledged program (to be supported by the crisis team, curiously) that would involve vendors, suppliers, and a distribution network to deliver expensive decorative live plants to the homes of thousands of workers. In the early peak of the global pandemic.

Ultimately, a voice of reason intervened to suggest a less resource-intensive gesture that could be provided with existing resources, didn't require crisis team support, and was more in line with the organization's identity as a responsible corporate citizen.

This is a simple story, but it underlines an important potential pitfall in crisis response. The stakeholders in question (this leadership team) felt powerless in their circumstances and struggled with their obligation to act. But in doing so, they lost sight of the broader priorities, painted by the story that the COVID-19 pandemic was only just beginning to tell. Meanwhile, the crisis team was working to prioritize the health and safety of workers, the integrity of sites, the continuity of product and service delivery, and the maintenance of critical functions. One can easily imagine how these circumstances could be amplified in more a high-stakes setting.

The challenge of balancing stakeholder perspectives, while putting the right priorities into action can be exceedingly difficult in complex crisis settings. The ability to be intentional about acting on priorities while also being sensitive to stakeholders is a fine line to walk. Having a program for managing action and information is a key tool for the crisis team.

How do I know what needs to be done?

When confronted with senior stakeholders who, for example, want to divert resources from a crisis response in earnest support of a secondary or completely unrelated task, how should the team respond? What should that conversation look like? In reality, it won't be simple. Ultimately teams need to support their stakeholders while managing responsible deployment of limited resources.

Part of the calculation lies in the fact that the question, "What needs to be done," can mean different things and has different answers.

First, it can be a question about task management: what tasks remain to be completed that haven't been done yet? This version of the question presupposes that there is no debate that the tasks in question need to be completed, and presumably in some sequence. There is assumed to be some order at work, and the question is simply clarifying arrangements. The answer to this question is reference to a project management framework, or even just a list. "Do this thing next, but not before this one is done."

It can also be a question about priorities: what needs doing now because we agree it is most important? This version of the question acknowledges an underlying order exists but is flexible and subject to change. An equilibrium has to be achieved between the actions that stakeholders *want* to take; those actions that *must* be taken (as a matter of life safety or survivability of the enterprise, for example); and the things that can actually be achieved with available time and resources. Ideally, all of this should occur while also incorporating feedback from the edges of the organization, as this book has discussed.

Some actions can be shaped by good initial response (recognition, escalation, open reporting from the edges of the organization). The organization's culture and the character of the crisis leadership will also influence the answer.

There are a lot of ways to tackle the problem of knowing what needs to be done, and some outstanding tools and methods are available. But one less commonly emphasized tool is the idea of sensemaking in the crisis response.

"What's the story here and now what do we do?"

Traditional approaches to objective setting and establishing priorities in crisis response tend to favor structured models, such as ICS and elements of the "Planning P." As previously discussed, these approaches are tested and work effectively in the right settings. Namely, where the circumstances meet with a familiar template for response.

This book has also talked about setting initial priorities based on one of these templates: focus first on life safety, incident stability, and protection of property/environment to the extent practical. Following from that is the reality that whatever is happening there will really only be a finite number of *effects* (as opposed to causes).

For the unconquerable organization, establishing the context around these issues can and should be part of rapid responsible escalation, and central to proceeding further with any attempt to answer, "What needs to be done."

Especially in highly complex commercial enterprises or production environments, after establishing these baseline parameters the question becomes, what next? In these sorts of contexts, the traditional models derived from emergency response and military practice may start to fall flat.

Returning to the early coronavirus example, in 2020 many large private sector companies in the US (and around the world) took the appropriate strategic decision to align their crisis responses with credible health authority guidance and requirements. For those companies in the US, this often meant following Centers for Disease Control (CDC) guidance. In doing so these organizations were able to define priorities for their responses that were linked to CDC recommendations, in a move that was quite sensible at the time for a variety of reasons. By May of 2020, many office-based commercial companies had transitioned to some form of remote reporting, had put workarounds for critical processes in place and were monitoring the day-to-day changes in the pandemic. In other words, their initial three objectives were covered (life safety in the workplace, incident stability in progress, and property/environment acknowledged) along with the "effects" related issues.

As the pandemic persisted in the ensuing months and year, however, some of those teams began to recognize that following health authority guidance alone, as a rule, was increasingly inadequate. The guidance at federal levels could seemingly contradict local requirements; sometimes the guidance was internally inconsistent or difficult to implement meaningfully; and at other times it was too broad or subject to change to be of use. It just wasn't working.

What some of these companies found was that to continue to meet their objectives of keeping people safe – while also continuing their business – they needed to contextualize the health authority guidance better. In some cases, this meant bringing together a diverse set of internal experts: medical and occupational health professionals, health and safety practitioners, facility managers, lawyers, representatives from business units, and so on. An ongoing series of conversations and debates followed which sought to clarify health authority guidance against the need for their specific business to meet or revise its own objectives while also ensuring that the health and safety of workers weren't compromised. Importantly, all of this had to be done in a rational, defensible, and ultimately understandable way. The conversation included – and was most informed by in some cases – the edges of the organization who would actually have to implement the actions being discussed.

Singular authoritative expertise had to give way to a collaborative, iterative conversation oriented around the question, "what is the story now and what do we have to do about it." The answer "follow CDC guidance" couldn't suffice when operations in San Diego or Chicago had differing and contradictory local requirements. This was compounded by the need to address site-specific business continuity needs or health conditions.

Sensemaking – a different way of setting priorities in crisis response

This in no way is intended to read as a criticism of CDC response to COVID-19. It is rather included as a recent illustration of what collective sensemaking in action can look like.

Sensemaking can play a role in early response, but life safety, immediate considerations for the protection of the environment or property, and some level of incident stability must be established first.

As discussed earlier, in unconquerable organizations sensemaking can be a powerful tool for identifying order where none exists or can be known. It doesn't have to be a formal or structured process – though it can be. In a 2015 study[1] of sensemaking among a leadership team in a real-world competitive crisis, researchers found that the sensemaking approach actually brought leader perceptions of what the response objectives should be into consensus. The response team in the study coalesced around key themes of strategic objectives from a very diverse set of concerns initially. The study also highlighted the importance of early identification and escalation, but showed that once that was achieved, the team learned and adapted to the unfolding crisis quickly through trial and error.

Once the initial standing objectives are understood, a cross functional team, working iteratively, can move very quickly toward figuring out what needs to be done next. In this way, the edges of the organization can be brought to bear on defining what "story" the crisis is telling. Essentially, the process of defining objectives becomes a team experience.

The elements of sensemaking, presented earlier, include:

- Scan the Immediate Landscape
- Seek Out Divergent Opinions
- Iterate by Testing Assumptions Continuously
- Adopt Multiple Perspectives
- Drive Iteration and Action

Some of this may sound flighty. Sensemaking simply represents the process that individuals and teams naturally follow in confronting complex circumstances. By giving it structure and meaning, a team can expedite the organic reasoning process and potentially accelerate it, rather than impose an arbitrary model to it (such as creating "SMART" objectives where they may not apply).

Above all, sensemaking is focused on action and organizing through communication. This is why it is considered a social process and an experience. The team engaged in collective sensemaking will move through phases of argument and expectation, where they give meaning to conditions by understanding what is contradictory and what is similar (just like the response teams trying to square CDC guidance with local rules and business needs). The team will derive from these discussions a set of actions based on committing to the meaning they have uncovered. As those actions return results — many of which will inevitably contradict the team's expectation, they will need to manipulate their action plan to respond to changes in the environment and new signals triggered by the action they are taking.

This takes the appearance of regular team meetings and sub team meetings — venues for conversation and joint experience — in which experiments are conducted in the form of actions and decisions. The outcome is a set of learnings. This collection of lessons becomes the "objective" set for the response. The team can use this experience as a point of reference for context in the past and direction in the unknown future:

> As a team we had to take these initial actions to ensure life safety and stabilize the response. From there, we recognized that the business had critical needs in remote sites, so we deployed resources X, Y, and Z. Those resources were consumed so fast that we needed to create a sub team to build a process for managing supply until a long term solution could be found. In the meantime, the crisis situation worsened, and we needed to change course. Knowing how fast resources would be used and how hard they were to find in the competitive environment, we decided instead to pivot out of that function.

In this way, the team begins to treat the problem as an experiment. Bear in mind, sensemaking is not concerned with certainty and getting it right the first time. It is about a continued rewriting of the emerging story in a way that makes it more complete and more inclusive of the newly available data and observations. The objective setting experience answers the question what things do we need to do; and sensemaking helps build the story which provided context. But how can this be put together in a way that is accessible — what is the "deliverable" of the sensemaking process in a crisis setting?

Build a map: iterative crisis action planning

One can google "crisis action plan" or "crisis management plan" and find quite literally thousands of templates and step-wise approaches or articles explaining the importance of such plans. Thin on the ground, however, are readily available examples of actual plans that went through a crisis. The reason for this probably has much to do with the fact that such plans would become highly sensitive once they are used in a real response. True enough, but it also leaves one wondering if there isn't another reason. Perhaps when the moment of crisis strikes, the team doesn't literally follow the plan. Perhaps they form something else along the way, using their plans to greater or lesser extents as they go.

To answer the question "What needs to be done" as part of responding to a crisis, the team needs to move from making sense to making meaning. Identifying where in the story the team and its stakeholders are is only a partial answer. Orientation without action is meaningless. Putting the context into action involves building some structure and putting decisions and tasks into motion. To achieve this – in conditions which will be defined in progress, where cause and effect are hard to correlate in real time – the team needs a map, more than a plan or a checklist. The sensemaking process serves such a need well because it continuously links past experience with the current situation and emerging presumptions about the future.

This step does not need to be complicated. The "map" is not a literal geographic representation. Although that can be part of it.

The map is the cumulative representation of where the team started, where it is now, and where it is going next. It represents the leadership direction and alignment; it connects the initial objectives that are complete; the objectives the team has established as part of the sensemaking process need to follow next; and allocates time and resource estimates. The map acknowledges that what occurred in the recent past may no longer be relevant, and what comes next may not be known.

In 2005, Peter Pirolli and Stuart Card presented an interesting study on sensemaking processes used by government intelligence analysts.[2] Their research explored the models used by intelligence analysts to bring structure to unstructured or diverse data sets, filter the information down and arrive at hypotheses for decision makers. As part of their research, they developed a notional model of a sensemaking loop in intelligence analysis.

The display builds upon Pirolli and Card's model and presents cognitive steps involved in the analysis of an unfolding crisis situation, reflected in two broad "loops." A model such as this can form the basis for understanding where the crisis team is in responding to an event. It is certainly not all-encompassing – but rather is intended to help guide the team in building their own map of the uncertainty that they are confronted with (Figure 7.1).

The "collecting/collating loop" entails bringing together available data (including from the edges of the organization) and narrowing down that information to a case or crisis-specific subset, referred to in Pirolli and Card as the "shoebox." This represents the information wrangling or marshalling of data that occurs in the early onset of crisis or whenever significant new events present. Sorting what is relevant from what is not – ensuring that key signals from operations filter through – is a critical early and ongoing process.

The collecting/collating loop will include the initial identification of a triggering event and any rapid escalation that takes place. The accumulation of any data or information at those stages will likely be unstructured and messy. It is necessary, therefore, to filter what is relevant from what is not; and from there to apply some simple structure, using the Clean Container concept. At this stage, the amount of effort invested in analysis and structure should be reasonably low and increase slowly at each level. This is because the relevance, value, and speed of information are determined more by the crisis than by the team itself. The information coming in may be likely to change faster than it can be processed. What matters most is ensuring that it gets filtered, rather than fully assessed.

The second loop, "the sensemaking loop," defines the process explained earlier for building and revising a working hypothesis or "story" of the unfolding situation. The outcome of this loop should be continuously reviewed mental models that adapt to new changes in data and circumstances. These should be treated as the basis for good, informed decisions.

Bear in mind, the whole set of steps is not as linear as it may appear here. Some critical information may demand immediate action without being boxed along the way. At the same time, it is important to remember that

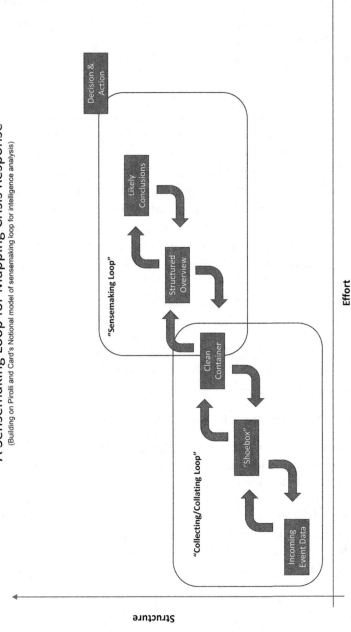

Figure 7.1 Sensemaking loop for mapping crisis response.

the process works downward, just as it moves upward. Decision-making, action, and likely conclusions will require additional information, new requests for support or clarification and evidence. The crisis team will navigate up and down the stages, but it is helpful to know where they are at any given time as it relates to an issue in order to remain properly oriented. In this way, the sensemaking loop forms the basis of a kind of map for the crisis response.

This map can take any number of forms, but a common, shared template is a good idea. There are a variety of crisis management technology tools available. Some of these may offer unique advantages in a given organization, but what they all likely have in common is that most people involved in a response will not have had contact with that technology since the last crisis or exercise. For that reason, it is worth considering a commonly available platform for tracking actions and status – any Office application, for example Excel, can work well. Everyone has access to it and some basic idea of how it works. Users don't need a special login or any training. There should be the least amount of additional friction imposed on the team and the response as possible.

The map should also contain a chronology of key events; a log of actions, owners, and status; and a centralized format for tracking resources.

"GETTING IT RIGHT"

"FCK": The Great KFC Chicken Crisis of 2018

In February 2018, nearly 800 of 900 KFC locations in the UK were closed for nearly a week following an unexpected supply chain crisis the company referred to as "operational issues."

What Happened? In the early morning hours of February 14, 2018, unrelated fatal and non-fatal vehicle accidents in different locations closed the M6 highway near several road junctions in Rugby, UK. Significantly, this area is home to the single DHL warehouse which had just become the new logistics partner for KFC, supplying the restaurant chain's entire supply of chicken for its UK operations. As soon as DHL delivery trucks departed their warehouse they were stopped in traffic. With nowhere to go, and with no other sources from which to supply ingredients, the chicken crisis started here. What followed were a cascading series of failures and difficulties – most of which were out of the KFC parent company's control – which brought the brand's reputation into immediate peril on social media and beyond.

The Fallout and Reaction. KFC responded rapidly with a creative and humorous marketing and public relations campaign featuring an empty KFC chicken bucket labeled "FCK," and accompanying social media messaging along the lines of "The Colonel is Working on it," "The Chicken Crossed the Road…," and #wheresmychicken. In doing so, the KFC team took an unequivocal business and supply chain disaster and turned it into a messaging and communications triumph.

What Can be Learned.

- KFC immediately recognized the severity of their supply chain crisis (though perhaps not its extent) as well as the likely damage to their brand online. By being quick from the start, KFC enabled itself to seize the advantage later in the communications battle.
- The team rapidly escalated and navigated through the unknown better as a result. DHL had literally just become their logistics partner; their previous logistics partner had six warehouses around the UK. There was no plan or playbook for this situation. They managed through Cynefin contexts from "chaotic" initially, through to "complex" and then "complicated."
- Until the supply chain could be restored there was little that could be done about the situation. For that reason, throughout the situation KFC focused on communications and conveyed openness, honesty, and sincerity. While their social media campaign made use of humor to great effect, it did not minimize the impact of the supply chain failure.
- Along those lines, KFC quickly and consistently managed its stakeholders, making sure they were identified and addressed properly and with sincerity.
- They championed their frontline employees. Not only did they recognize its chain store workers as impacted stakeholders who were themselves experiencing a hardship because of the circumstances, they elicited their input in managing the impact to customers. They also provided national recognition to their workers to show appreciation for the work they did "on the front lines" of the chicken crisis.
- Lastly, the management team remained oriented or "mapped" to what was happening for the duration of the "crisis," approximately a week of service interruption.

"GETTING IT RIGHT"

The 2013 Superbowl Blackout

What Happened? On February 3, 2013, Superbowl XLVII between the Baltimore Ravens and San Francisco 49ers was in progress at the Mercedes-Benz Superdome in New Orleans. Moments into the second half, a partial power outage impacted the stadium power supply, plunging the crowd and players into partial darkness and pausing the game for 34 minutes.

Response and Reaction. By pure coincidence at the moment when the power went out, CBS reporter Armen Keteyian was present in the stadium command center with a camera crew finishing an interview with the head of NFL game day operations, Frank Supovitz. Keteyian kept the cameras rolling as Supovitz and his team leapt into action. The team can be seen on the footage from that day working through the problem:

Operations: "We've lost the A feed."

"What does that mean?" Supovitz asked.

"We have to use the bus tie."

"WHAT DOES THAT MEAN?"

"That means about a 20-minute delay." And so on.

What Can be Learned. The thing that stands out about the Superbowl blackout, aside from the calm demeanor of the NFL command center team, is the process they followed. They naturally fell into a rapid and organic sensemaking activity. It is not apparent from the video, but the team in the command center knew with a fair amount of certainty that they weren't experiencing a deliberate attack. In other words, they recognized the obvious power failure but also ruled out a security or imminent safety threat quickly.

That meant that although they didn't know what the cause was (it turned out to be an unexpected equipment failure outside the stadium), they didn't need to move to an immediate life-saving posture, managing an evacuation or law enforcement response. Instead, they were able to prioritize the need to get a message to the thousands of people in the stadium, and continually update it. The content of that message, and other decisions, would depend on the time needed to restore power. That is apparent in the back and forth in the dialogue above: operations providing detail to command – but a conversation defining the salient points for the collective team to make a decision. The drive is for meaning and action. "What do we need to do now?" Again, the team moved from Cynefin contexts quickly and seamlessly, without strict reference to a plan or playbook.

From establishing sensemaking as part of the action planning and response process; and orienting to the "story" of the unfolding crisis; the responding team also needs to coordinate its activities with elements of the team and various stakeholders. This is a key part of the "what needs to be done" approach for unconquerable organizations.

Assembling response sessions: what works and what doesn't

Convening meetings and briefings is a key task in crisis response, a skill for crisis leaders and coordinators, and at times also a challenge to the response itself. There is no way to manage a response without convening teams of people to coordinate what needs to be done, how and by whom.

There are many approaches to conducting good meetings and briefings available – some of which are specific to crisis or emergency management. There is a lot of good advice online about how to run "great crisis meetings." As well, traditional systems like ICS offer terrific tools and templates for such settings. The challenge can be adopting a new system on the fly and trying to follow the template rather than focusing on the issues at hand. On the other hand, where the organizational context calls for it, such formality or procedure is entirely necessary and called for.

Almost any format will work, if it is as near to the normal or usual format for meetings at the organization as practical. Introducing new processes or formalities during an ongoing crisis can introduce friction, which is the opposite of what good crisis meetings should do. In other words, the meeting itself shouldn't introduce new or unfamiliar ceremony to an already unfamiliar and unstable situation. This is particularly true for organizations where most of the stakeholders are not engaged with day to day resilience work or may have little direct experience with crisis responses.

Instead, crisis meetings should be treated as part of the process of asking and answering the three big questions, but most especially "what needs to be done," followed, of course, by "who's doing what."

The purpose of any team gathering in a crisis should be reasonably well defined, accessible (without unnecessary or unfamiliar ceremony or formality), and disciplined. This is an area for blue sky planning which, like rapid responsible escalation, is worth investing in and training for.

Types of gatherings

It can be useful to think in terms of the different types of gatherings that may be necessary, each with its own time and place.

- Briefings: Gatherings that are less interactive, informational, directive, and limited in scope.
- Meetings: Settings that are more interactive, drive sensemaking and coordination.

At the outset of a crisis, an Initial Briefing is always recommended. The agenda for the initial briefing can be derived from the crisis leader's Time Out meeting and should strictly present facts without conjecture. Whereas the leader's Time Out is an opportunity for the initially responding team to align among themselves, the Initial Briefing should be viewed as the first opportunity for the team to align (and set expectations with) key stakeholders who are not directly involved in the immediate response. This can include senior leaders, functional and support units, internal business partners, etc.

This Initial Briefing can include the following:

- An overview of the current situation.
  Establish the status of life safety concerns, the status of organization key assets, or any environmental impact. Address whether the incident is stabilized, is continuing to escalate, or whether it cannot be known.
- Summarize the initial objectives and focus.
  Beyond the life safety, property/environment and stability objectives, has the team identified any other immediate objectives concerning critical assets for the organization.
- Characterize the response.
  Define what elements of the organization are engaged in the response already (for example, Security, Safety, Facility Management, and Local Operations); define whether any outside partners or agencies are involved (law enforcement, first responders, regulators, government agencies, competitors, suppliers).
- Address resource limits and requirements.
  At a very high level, address what resources are already engaged, enroute, or requested but not received. If a critical resource is known

to be unavailable, specify that as a constraint to the response (i.e. lack of fuel supplies or utility service will slow the ability of operations to resume key functions).

• End with a commitment for the next briefing.
   Provide a specific time/place for the next update in the near future, along with a commitment to attempt to address open questions in the interim. It may not be possible to address all stakeholder concerns, but it is critical to hear and track these questions to closure – even if they can't be answered immediately.

It is worth remembering that the initial briefing (or any subsequent briefing) is not a press conference; and it is not a brainstorming session or debate. Rather, it is a key step in establishing management control over the crisis, bringing some order to the appearance of chaos, gaining acceptance of the approach the team will take (and displaying a measure of discipline in the process), and providing assurance to stakeholders that the response will be orderly and effective.

After an initial briefing is complete, it is important to establish a regular cadence of ongoing briefings early on – even if it is not clear how long the situation will continue. Subsequent ongoing briefings should follow a similar agenda to the initial brief, but as the response evolves it should involve report outs from the key response functions. To be seen as valuable, the agenda for the briefings should remain focused and crisp. The shorter the briefing, often, the better. The purpose is to quickly status progress against objectives, and surface or identify issues, and not to solve problems. Briefings should occur with enough regularity that they offer meaningful updates and contact between responders. A way to measure this is by the number of emails and phone calls they save. If the team can avoid providing constant on-demand updates to stakeholders by instead instilling the confidence in them that the next update will be concise but comprehensive enough to answer their questions, they have done a good job. Each briefing should always conclude with a commitment on when the next briefing will occur, even if it is already scheduled. A disciplined approach to briefing can provide situational awareness to a broader set of stakeholders, even in complex and quickly changing situations. At the same time, orderly regular briefings help turn down the volume of noise in the organization, reducing the chaos and uncertainty that discussion around the incident, whatever it is, will create.

Whereas briefings are a setting where information is conveyed, updates are delivered, and Q&A is limited and focused on clarifying understanding, response team meetings are where the rubber meets the road.

The response team cannot achieve its goals of collective sensemaking, revising objectives, and tracking actions from briefings alone. The venue for the collaboration that must occur among the response team – and the edges of the organization – is in working sessions and meetings. These sessions have the specific goal of driving the iterative sensemaking process: an open, collaborative and dynamic setting. These discussions will result in the more definitive updates that can be communicated in somewhat more formal briefings. The working sessions and meetings should involve players with direct involvement in finding solutions or imagining them.

A word about intelligence in crisis response

The paradigm for crisis management put forth here involves sensemaking – probing, sensing, experimenting – and considers formalizing the things that we as people begin to do intuitively in unstructured and complex conditions. These ideas are also predicated on the notion described earlier that the outcome of every crisis will be a combination of successes and failures, never all one or the other. Consequently, every crisis response is composed of hundreds of little decisions and actions each of which represents a learning opportunity. Whereas traditional planning may fall short against today's complex crises, an approach that values learning and experimentation presents opportunity. In this way, planning is learning – for the unconquerable organization.

Another way to think about this is that crisis response can fundamentally be an intelligence-led activity.

At a fundamental level, "what needs to be done" depends entirely on what is happening, how conditions are changing, and which actions can lead to solutions. It is common in crisis responses for information to take on a life of its own: people hoard it, control it, seek to overwhelm with it, are overwhelmed by it, and generally circulate it with reckless abandon. Managing the information flow is important, and a key activity of the crisis team.

Recognizing the difference between information and intelligence is also important. Especially as it relates to a critical operation, where the anomalies that preceded the crisis started at the edges of the organization, the context for solutions starts there as well. The difference between "information" and "intelligence" is context. The *information* may be an equipment reading. The *intelligence* is the implication of that reading on the decision that needs to be made. Intelligence is information which has value because it brings meaning. Information without meaning and context in a crisis is dead weight.

In traditional terms there is an intelligence cycle that repeats through stages of planning, direction, collection, collation, analysis, production, and dissemination. Not every crisis situation allows for this pattern. And in practice, not every intelligence shop adheres to it — especially in fast moving situations. However, it is worth keeping in mind that more information is not necessarily better. Qualified information — information with meaningful context that can be explored by the team (even in a fast paced setting) — that's intelligence. One of the ways to promote rapid responsible escalation and promote the support of internal partners is to remind them of this distinction, and of their role in defining what becomes intelligence in a crisis.

These things ultimately move the needle toward success in response. And this approach, in combination with other factors, helps guide the team in clarifying what needs to be done, fast. Information that can be made into intelligence links the "collecting/collating loop" to the "sensemaking loop" and drives the whole team more quickly to good decisions.

TAKEAWAYS

Through proper management of information and the sensemaking process, unconquerable organizations have the ability to know *what needs to be done* at any given time in a crisis response.

This book discussed the importance of rapid and responsible escalation as one of the critical steps in moving from early recognition of a potential crisis to initial responses. Companies that perform best in crises execute this step well. One of the important considerations for good execution in the early stages is tracking actions and resources.

At the earliest stages, record keeping and tracking actions are not the most critical priority. This is where the *clean container* comes in. Use less effort and less structure, keep it simple now, so it can be kept simple later. If an incident escalates to a level of significant severity, the ability to quickly status actions in progress vs actions completed will become critical.

Key considerations for action management: What do I want to do, what do I have to do, what can I do? What am I trying to accomplish here?

Incorporate sensemaking as a part of the action planning and management process. Use it to develop a "map" of where the team is in the unfolding story being told by the crisis.

Establish a pattern of meetings and briefings in a regular cadence to build a structure around the response.

Think about distinguishing between intelligence and information. Let intelligence – that information that has contextual value – inform the sensemaking loop and inform good decisions.

Notes

1. Ian A. Combe and David J. Carrington "Leaders' sensemaking under crises: Emerging cognitive consensus over time within management teams," The Leadership Quarterly, Vol. 26, 2015, pp. 307–322.
2. Peter Pirollo and Stuart Card, "The Sensemaking Process and Leverage Points for Analyst Technology as Identified Through Cognitive Task Analysis," Conference: Proceedings of International Conference on Intelligence Analysis, January 2005.

8

"WHO'S DOING WHAT?" – THE MAPMAKERS

Crisis teams and responders

Knowing who's in charge and what needs to be done are key parts of the unconquerable equation. The third leg of the pedestal has to do with "who's doing what?" The answer to this question involves two main points: how crisis teams move into action; and how the right parts and pieces of the organization integrate to bring sense to unstable or escalating situations (i.e. "joint sensemaking").

The value that a crisis team brings can be measured by its ability to not only overcome the story that the crisis is telling, but also to hurdle the obstacles presented by the organization itself to achieve the necessary objectives. In other words, unconquerable organizations establish teams that can buck the systems of everyday operations to protect the most essential functions. Critically, they achieve this without compromising their values, the law or the well-being of their own people.

It is a delicate balance. Striking it can be achieved by returning to the analogy of the crisis team as mapmakers. At the start of the crisis, the available options may be too few or too many to properly

DOI: 10.4324/9781003216803-11

operationalize. The crisis team in the unconquerable organization brings focus to an unfolding narrative, building a map of the events in the recent past, the actions that are unfolding, and anticipating the general direction to follow.

Consider these real-world examples:

On February 24, 2022, Russian President Vladimir Putin announced a "special military operation" in eastern Ukraine effectively beginning the invasion of the country by the tens of thousands of Russian soldiers staged around Ukrainian borders. In the days and weeks to follow, NATO allies imposed crippling economic sanctions against Russia, multinational corporations closed their operations in both countries, and Russia quickly became isolated from the rest of the world. A humanitarian tragedy unfolded in Ukraine, while political instability and groaning economic uncertainty proliferated globally.

The terrible loss of civilian life and devastation in Ukraine cannot be ignored. Around the world, the crisis teams at every large company with a presence in Russia, Ukraine, or both, were pressed into action. Most teams had already been monitoring the simmering situation for some time before open hostility began. Many global companies had workforces in Ukraine in need of immediate assistance. But they also had workforces in Russia who were confronted with ominous new risks, including loss of access to many Western brands and services as well as the sudden decline in economic conditions following sanctions imposed by the rest of the world. There were critical operations and customers to consider in both countries, especially for those companies that deliver life-saving products or critical services such as medicines, food, and energy. There were also, of course, broader questions about the impacts to supply chains, longer term economic conditions, and geopolitical risks.

On April 17, 2018, Southwest Airlines Flight 1380 from New York to Dallas was traveling at 30,000 feet when an engine exploded, causing shrapnel to break a window. Passenger Jennifer Riordan was pulled headfirst partly out of the window. The plane made an emergency landing in Philadelphia, but Ms. Riordan did not survive. Before the plane was on the ground, the crisis went public in real time, live on social media as passengers onboard the aircraft posted messages, photos, and video online. Southwest Airlines was confronted with the first death of a passenger on a US flight since 2009, the first fatality on a Southwest flight in its history, and storm of viral social media rapidly escalating around the event.

Meanwhile, in a conference room in Dallas, TX, Southwest senior executives had gathered for a scheduled leadership development conference when phones around the room blared an alert from the company's crisis communications system. Their crisis response plan had been activated – a plan they had recently exercised, and which had seen some real-world action with three recent hurricanes requiring significant coordination in the past year. But no one had been prepared for the possibility of a passenger death, in such a terrible and unexpected way. The team was quick to act, had a culture of readiness and moved right away toward establishing initial objectives.

———————————

In August 2016, Samsung unveiled its much-anticipated new smartphone, the Galaxy Note 7 to fawning reviews and great excitement among Android users. The device was poised to steal market share from major competitors like Apple, and boasted an improved camera, a better screen, faster processor, and improved battery life. On August 24th, however, the first of what would become many reports emerged on social media that the device batteries were overheating, burning, and even exploding. The reports were accompanied by images of smoldering or charred Samsung devices. Eventually, reports began to claim that the devices weren't just overheating, they were exploding like bombs.

By many accounts, the response from Samsung was a fiasco. A tepid initial response failed to acknowledge the true scope or potential risk posed to the company or its customers. On September 2, 2016, the company announced a voluntary global recall of 2.5 million devices, citing the faulty battery issue, and started an "exchange program" in which consumers were offered a replacement device. Then, when the replacement devices started exploding too, Samsung still didn't halt production, but instead continued to offer replacement devices, claiming they were safe. Ultimately, regulators and other stakeholder intervened. US airlines very publicly banned Samsung devices on flights, and the US Consumer Product Safety Commission instructed consumers to stop using the phones in a September 15 US product recall. The impact on Samsung's reputation and bottom line, at a critical moment in the company's evolution, was substantial.

Once the scope and impact became apparent, how did these teams respond? How did they organize to support the safety and well-being of their workers and their customers? As well, how did these teams ensure the continuity of their critical operations (especially in cases where those operations were a matter of life safety for users or customers)? What other unforeseen challenges did they have to confront?

The answers to these questions involve building a crisis team of "mapmakers." To achieve this the unconquerable organization needs to get the right team together, fast; establish a "team of teams;" be sure to connect to the edges of the organization; and integrate efficiently.

Getting the right team, fast: activating

In each of the cases above, the real impact to organizations is experienced as something unexpected. Some may have anticipated military action against Ukraine by Russia, but most in the private sector could not have predicted exactly what it would be like to confront it. For Southwest, crisis response is a well-established part of their culture and has been used in real world incidents and exercises. But the reality of a mid-air tragedy – even if they have imagined it in a planning scenario – is much different. For Samsung, a product defect escalated into a recall and eventually into a full-blown global reputational disaster. With each passing week, another shoe kept dropping on Samsung, who seemed slow to orient to the story that was unfolding before them. The "unexpected-ness" of crisis is present in every case – even those that a team has practiced for.

Organizations that are quick off the starting line, escalate quickly and establish objectives early on will perform better in crisis. Maintaining the momentum requires getting a team in place to start acting on the work that needs to be done and build the map.

The right crisis team needs to be multidisciplinary: not only in terms of staff position, but also in terms of expertise and exposure to the crisis management process. The team has to take the shape of its container. Some crises might call for an emphasis on communications and social media expertise. Others may depend heavily on a specific operational or engineering skill set. For this reason, blue-sky planning should look to enable a set of core standing crisis team roles who act as the primary responders and a roster or stable of key subject matter experts who can bring specific expertise to bear quickly.

The core crisis team

The core standing crisis team comprises a set of roles which are likely to be necessary in almost any response. This team usually consists of a small number of people whose primary role involves responsibility for crisis management at the organization. In this way, the standing team becomes the process guardians for the crisis management approach that additional members who join the team will be become a part of. This group will commonly be the first responders to a crisis, will establish the basic framework, provide counsel and support to business leaders, hand off crisis leadership to senior leadership in some cases, and provide direct support to the Crisis Command Team (more to follow). It is also often this team that will assess the need for further escalation as conditions worsen.

A Core Crisis Team can consist of the following members, at a bare minimum:

- Crisis Team Lead: Activates the team, and establishes initial objectives.
- Coordinator: Identifies and notifies stakeholders of initial assessments; tracks and directs team activity.
- Communications Lead: Begins establishing decision gates for messaging and content.

In smaller organizations, or for smaller initial responses the Team Lead and Coordinator can be the same person. But as a situation escalates they should be separated as roles.

As a crisis escalates, the team will need to track what needs to be done and what the unfolding narrative means to begin sensemaking. The next two roles for the standing team are specialists:

- Assessment and Info Management: Maintains a current situation assessment and processes incoming inquiries.
- Action and Tracking Management: Manages the tracking of actions, resources, and assignments.

Again, in small organizations or in contained crises these roles can probably be combined, but as the situation escalates it is preferable to separate them. These five core functions provide the backbone for the subsequent team members to work from as they join the response.

Internal strategic partners

As a matter of blue-sky planning, the Standing Team should have a roster of available internal strategic partners ready to support the crisis team in the initial response phase. This should include representation from every major business unit in the organization, and representatives should be decision makers who can direct resources and teams to support the response. This is the group of decision makers who can deploy the Crisis Management Envoy from within their part of the organization. The crisis team should not be in the situation where they need to maintain an enormous inventory of hundreds of internal specialists and SME's. Instead, the roster should reference senior leaders who are briefed on the readiness culture, aware of the crisis response culture, and partnered in advance to work with internal specialists as needed. These leaders do not need to be crisis response experts or provided with extensive training. They simply need an understanding of the process and be provided with a clear request that they can meet when the moment arrives.

This way the crisis team only needs to approach a small number of key leaders to request resources (ideally through a network of Crisis Management Envoys), rather than chase potentially outdated contacts from a constantly changing list.

The advantage of this approach is that it acts as a notification to stakeholders and a request for assistance simultaneously. It enlists the organization in engaging a solution that will work for them. It ensures that the organization obtains the right expertise quickly and delivers it to the team, rather than the crisis team spending time searching for them. This is all part of ensuring that the crisis response begins to take the shape of its container.

First response by role

Getting this done fast is another area where planning pays off (like rapid, responsible escalation). Think "first responses, not first responders." Teams that practice an activation process see better results. There are a variety of great technologies available for notification and activation of crisis teams, but the technology does not need to be complex. What matters most is there is a core team whose responsibilities are understood (and it is understood what they are not responsible for); and that there is a small set of strategic partners in an orbit around that team.

All of this needs to be highly tailored to the organization, but that is where the real value of planning and exercising comes in. Those activities should focus on clarifying "first response by role." It can be very hard to prescribe action in advance of crisis. This is a point of failure – or at least lost productivity – in a lot of traditional planning activities. However, the investment is worthwhile in evaluating what each member of the crisis team – including the strategic partners on the SME roster – should do first (and, maybe, second) in response to a team activation. While actual response activities will vary according to conditions, the first several actions are likely to always be the same.

As with the response escalation protocol, this will necessarily be highly specific to the organization. For example, the crisis team leader's "first responses" may include, establishing affirmative contact with the Core team, calling in additional crisis staff, assessing the risk of escalation, and establishing a cadence for initial and subsequent briefings. The Communications Lead's "first responses" may include, for example, pulling relevant holding statement/templates, assigning aides to handling incoming inquiries, and compiling initial internal talking points. Whatever these are for the specific organization may be worth documenting, then challenging in exercises to refine them.

Southwest could not have imagined what would occur on Flight 1380. But their planning and exercising supported a culture that made fast, transparent, and effective response possible. Without knowing what the next hours or days would bring, the team built a map of what was taking place that they were able to use to orient themselves as the crisis unfolded.

The team of teams: integrating for action

Having an initial team that can stand up quickly following the recognition of a crisis is critical to good outcomes. However, the initial team will also be quickly overwhelmed by expanding and escalating circumstances. Good crisis response isn't won by a crisis team alone. The real answer to the question, "Who's doing What" is a Team of Teams (Figure 8.1).

Once the initial briefing, assessment, and early responses have been complete, the team will likely need to settle in for a longer haul. For good outcomes, and for maximum benefit from the edges of the organization, it can be helpful to structure a response organization in a few layers.

This can quickly become elaborate. It need not be. Less is more and simple is better. The key is making the most of the existing organization

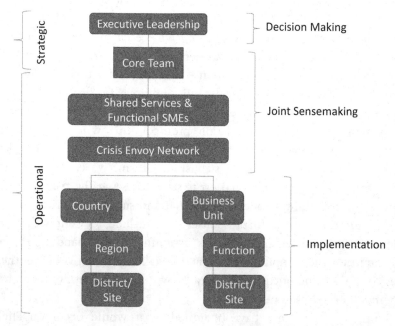

Figure 8.1 "Team of teams" structure.

to the extent possible, and mirroring the crisis organization to it at a high level. In basic terms this means there should be a strategic team responsible for major decision-making and accountability. This is typically the senior most executive team in a large enough crisis. There should also be a larger team of responders handling the implementation of operational and tactical, day-to-day activities.

These two functions are very different, and it can be helpful to stratify them with an intermediate level. Bringing together the owners of the decisions and the people who have to live with their decisions can sometimes be difficult. In the center, the core team, supported by a set of relevant critical shared services representatives (Security, IT, HR, Finance, Logistics, Legal) and the crisis envoy network, represent the rubber meeting the road. The deliverable for this team is twofold: this is where the joint sensemaking takes place (not in the board room, and not in operations); and this is where the decisions that need to be made are identified before being presented up. This level should bring the representation from across the organization to the crisis team, distilled and translated through the Envoys in the most direct fashion.

Where this sensemaking team identifies critical needs, they should not burden themselves with finding solutions. This team should look to offload task forces and subteams to chase specific issues and return to the central team with proposals for consideration in the big picture. For example, the Samsung organization eventually developed a Battery Advisory Group of technical experts to review the then unknown causes of the exploding batteries. This is not a task that a central crisis team could achieve in addition to everything else. Similarly, in the COVID-19 response many corporate crisis teams needed to spin off sub-teams to evaluate specific facility safety issues, employment law matters, research new protective measures, and so on. Ideally, sub-teams can also focus on business unit specific needs where they exist. The point is authority for finding solutions needs to be delegated down as far as reasonable in crisis settings. This means allowing experts to focus sensemaking activities on their areas, where discrete issues exist and then reinsert their findings into the broader mapmaking process. Understand, the overall crisis (e.g. the early days of COVID-19) may be complex in the Cynefin sense of the word. Within that context there may be questions that are "complex," which can be clarified through expert analysis among lawyers or doctors or health and safety experts, for example. The full crisis team does not need to participate in every one of those discussions as long as there is connectivity between teams.

The social process of crisis response exists not only among individuals, but among teams of individuals. The deployment of focused sub teams is a very effective strategy for keeping the response focused, lean, and on pace with events.

Who's doing what?

This book argues that bringing in the edges of the organization can make the difference in crisis outcomes. That depends on a lot of factors, some of which can be built into the organization when a crisis isn't ongoing. Knowing who's doing what, however, acknowledges that "everyone" can't participate in the crisis response. That isn't possible, or helpful. The intent is for channels of feedback to exist. A process for interpreting that feedback and integrating all kinds of incoming signals is essential to the response. But being unconquerable also does not mean leaving the edges of the organization to fend for themselves. The answer to who's doing what also includes who's accountable for what.

LOSING THE MAP

Stora Enso is one of the living companies celebrated by Arie de Geus for their highly unbossed, decentralized approach to management and innovation. It has been recognized as a key reason for their centuries of longevity – the company's continuous operations date back to the 1300 AD. Part of the reason for that was the delegation of responsibility to people closest to operations, and the giving of ownership of issues to those on the edges. This practice was always positively received in the business. What happens, though, if the center loses the overview of what is actually taking place? Between 2008 and 2014, Stora Enso experienced three significant scandals that nearly shattered their reputation. In 2008, the company was openly accused of double book-keeping its operations in North America. The accounting scandal caused the company to be trashed in European media, an event followed by an incoherent communications strategy on the part of the company. In 2012 a documentary criticizing the company's land leasing practices in China claimed Stora Enso had intimidated local land owners and illegally grabbed land. Two years later, a 2014 documentary revealed child labor in the supply chain in Pakistan. Naturally, stakeholders were enraged, customers and investors fled, and Stora's reputation was in tatters.

In the years that followed, the company found that their decentralized approach had introduced risks that weakened their controls against these issues. It appeared that local and regional risk assessments were frequently distilled on their way up the chain.

It also appeared that top management was not well equipped to handle these types of crises. They had never faced many of these issues. Priority was driven to localized responses, but many of the issues were beyond local authority to address – especially those where the media, reputation, and centralized practices were concerned. Local operations were unable to see the broader picture but were expected to respond. Consequently, garbled versions of the truth on the ground were filtered up the chain. And inconsistency between messaging coming from the central management, local divisions, and regional management prevailed. These breakdowns eventually escalated into urgent customer and investor issues.

Stora Enso may have taken some of their ambitions around decentralizing management a bit too far. In response to these situations, the company had to consciously reign in the centralized planning of some of their activities. As a practical matter, there are sometimes limits and tradeoffs with integrating and decentralizing response management. The reader will have to judge the context of their own organization to determine the right level of centralized control.

It is with this in mind that it is important to be intentional about structuring the crisis response into a team of teams, but always with a core team at the center providing the guiding hand, championing company values, and ensuring that the map is being made, and the story that is being told is truthful and accurate.

Treating the problem as an experiment and making everyone (not literally "everyone," but the members of the broad crisis response) problem owners can be done and can achieve better outcomes. The development of a strong crisis management envoys network can aid in doing this responsibly, without introducing new risks into the environment.

TAKEAWAY

The answer to "who's doing what" consists of two main components: how crisis teams move into action; and how the right parts and pieces of the organization integrate to bring sense to unstable or escalating situations (i.e. "joint sensemaking").

Organizations that are quick off the starting line, escalate quickly and establish objectives early on will perform better in crisis. Maintaining the momentum requires getting a team in place to start acting on the work that needs to be done and build the map.

It seems obvious, but as a matter of blue-sky planning, obtaining clarity around roles for a core crisis team and key internal stakeholders will accelerate the initial response and result in better outcomes. This can't be achieved as effectively while the crisis is in motion.

Establish first responses by role, instead of first responders. Less is more and simple is better. Make the most of the existing organization to the extent possible, and mirror the crisis organization to it at a high level. Build a strategic team responsible for major decision-making and accountability, supported by a larger team of responders handling the implementation of operational and tactical, day-to-day activities.

9

CONCLUSION

Becoming unconquerable

Every crisis is a call to action. The origin of the word – a moment of decision – resonates within anyone it touches and demands action. The implication is that we do not come out the same as we went in. There will be wins *and* losses in every response. The outcome of the crisis is always a combination – never a total victory or loss. That means that planning can't be thought of as an activity that is "completed" at some point in an annual cycle.

Annual planning cycles are a fine way of managing the administrative aspects of a crisis program during normal business conditions. But they alone are not enough, particularly if they do not acknowledge crises as an opportunity for growth or change. For that reason, traditional planning alone is not equivalent to readiness. Any strategist can tell you the only thing an organization can truly plan is the opening move; everything else follows organically from there.

True readiness comes from the people in an organization working together under a common set of values. When the unexpected happens,

DOI: 10.4324/9781003216803-12

organizations that thrive do so because they can flex and adapt on the fly. For these organizations, "planning" is learning. And that never stops.

Like planning, resilience alone is not enough. It is the nature of crisis to surprise, frustrate, disrupt, and disorder attempts to control it. Plans and resilience suffice until the crisis acts against them; then they start to deteriorate.

Resilience is an increasingly popular term, especially in the post-COVID-19 world. Every organization claims to have it or need more of it. One generally thinks of resilience as a positive thing, the capacity of a person or organization to bounce back or to persevere. The growth of organizational resilience as a practice in many businesses is a good thing as well. However, survey results like the PwC Global Crisis Survey, question if the effort is properly directed: far less than half of the respondents had a relevant plan in place, many felt their plans were inadequate, and very few (20%) felt their organizations were in a better place in March 2021 than before the start of the pandemic. These findings are not unique to PwC's survey, and many practitioners probably know these things intuitively about their own organizations.

There is a tremendous opportunity for well-constructed and perhaps revised crisis management approaches in complex organizations. More than ever, crisis management is a source of value for organizations in the post-pandemic era. Those who properly apply their crisis management programs are likely to uncover new potential in their business and among their people.

This book is about becoming unconquerable as an enterprise. Crisis management is not – and should never be – an individual exercise. The proposed alternative here is to build strength by organizing for readiness and developing broad competencies across disciplines in the organization. The truth is that no one person can single-handedly save the day, and even good teams need to work within the confines of their organizations to be effective in crisis. The intent of this book is to offer pragmatic options for tackling this challenge.

Many of today's crisis management practices are derived from military, law enforcement, and public sector sources, with good reason. However, many of these approaches are losing relevance, or are being challenged in today's increasingly complex, but less hierarchical organizations which are confronted with new kinds of risks.

It is also true that organizations in crisis can emerge stronger, and crisis can be experienced as a form of growth. The challenge is making it through the early stages of the crisis well enough to find the opportunity it presents. This is where becoming unconquerable starts. Companies that perform best in crisis execute on these four things:

- Recognize triggering events quickly.
- Focus on initial objectives and practice iterative leadership.
- Always appropriately address stakeholders, and above all
- Accept the unknowability and uncertainty of their circumstances.

Doing these things well in times of crisis means that in times of calm the leadership is adaptive to circumstances; willing to pivot into uncharted areas; willing to loosen centralized control; and define for themselves a clear identity. As noted, this may not be possible in every organization, for example where centralized control is a favored part of the culture.

Even in settings where the culture is less permissive of loosened control, it is still possible for a crisis team to drive good decisions, help leaders lead, and even identify new opportunities. They can achieve this by bringing the story of the crisis situation to life in the present, building an unfolding map of the circumstances it is presenting, and guiding iterative decision-making from the beginning. Most importantly, those in operations at the edges of the organization must be linked to the crisis management team and welcomed into joint sensemaking.

As a practical matter, readiness happens on "blue-sky days." For the unconquerable organization, the blue-sky day objective should be readiness on a collective level. Having teams of empowered staff and leaders who value agility and are willing to be adaptive, rather than dogmatic, takes skill and commitment.

Reaching this goal takes individual effort, especially on the part of leadership and the crisis team. But it is not their responsibility alone. Their task is also to create the conditions for growth of crisis competencies among all members of the organization. Among other things, this is what it takes to unboss the response capability.

This way, when the moment of crisis comes, the team and the organization are better positioned to respond from a place of strength. By executing the four elements mentioned above, the responding team can manage initial complexity. What matters most is:

- Frontline operations are trusted to recognize emerging patterns that deviate significantly from the norm.
- Frontline managers are trusted to orient to these patterns and begin to construct a recommendation independently.
- Senior leadership and the core crisis team are responsive to these inputs and actively resist the tendency to increase friction or hinder interaction.

Doing these things becomes simpler when we think in terms of effect, rather than causes. Regardless of cause, the effects of an incident will always, only be the unexpected unavailability of people, places, or things. To program for this kind of readiness, a tailored but adaptive rapid escalation protocol can serve an organization well. Responsible escalation protocols should prioritize detecting, assessing, and reporting anomalies with speed and accuracy – but without sending the organization into chaos. Paired with a network of Crisis Envoys to carry the message, the local operations and edges of the organization can be powerfully and meaningfully knit into the core crisis response.

This approach can be practiced and improved over time with good blue-sky planning and "premortem" exercises, while always keeping in mind the key response imperatives: first, protect life, then stabilize the incident, and then protect property/environment.

Crises are a time when other than normal leadership is required. "Crisis leaders" do not have to hold a title or a position (though it helps if they do as a result of good blue-sky planning). Experience helps, but it need not be a prerequisite. The crisis leader is a servant leader – someone who can motivate a broad population of experts and responders, and galvanize their vision for what needs to be done into practical action.

The crisis leader helps the team bring clarity and stability to situations where there is none. They favor exploration over certainty and are willing to allow a sensemaking process to work in a way that creates a map of what is really taking place. This is why unconquerable organizations can define what needs to be done at any given time in the response. One way of organizing for providing good decisions and appropriate action while the crisis is ongoing is to pattern activity for the crisis team around the idea of a "collecting/collating" loop and a "sensemaking" loop.

This map becomes a real-time playbook for managing the ongoing incident, and it often starts with a "clean container." In other words, a simple framework that allows the team, their partners, and stakeholders to ask and answer three key questions at any time: Who's in Charge, What needs to be Done, and Who's Doing What?

One last question: what next?

My hope is that you have found something in these pages to provoke ideas or questions about the crisis management approach in your organization. It may be the case that traditional approaches serve your organization well and will continue to. In which case, if it ain't broke don't fix it.

On the other hand, there may be concepts or even fragments of ideas here that can help you start off a conversation or lead and counsel your own teams and stakeholders in a different way.

There is no doubt that the world around us is changing in new and surprising ways. The patterns of crisis in the last decade have shown an escalating frequency and complexity of issues. I believe this trend will persist, and as it does, crisis teams will be called upon more often to respond to less familiar problems. In order to succeed and to be of value, we are going to need to execute well on the things we see most often: security incidents, natural disasters, operational disruptions. But we will also need to be willing to support our organizations and clients as they confront new challenges that we may not have playbooks for.

This will be uncomfortable. We're going to have to get ready.

I also believe that these changes put crisis teams in the very unique position of being able to influence our organizations to see the opportunities that come with unexpected, unfortunate events. We can do well by doing good. To the extent we can help leaders and stakeholders see that perspective when they aren't able to, we should. Experience shows that some organizations learn the most after going through something tough. Let's help them make the most of bad situations, and in doing so bring out the best in their people and communities.

THANKS AND ACKNOWLEDGMENTS

This book was only possible through the support of many people, whether they know it or not. Above all, I am blessed with a wonderful and supportive family. I also benefit from a strong community of true friends and colleagues. My friends and family are the people who have seen me through so many joyful moments and chapters of my life; and they are the people who come together when times aren't so good and help each other through. The generosity and love they have shown me and one another over the years has been a powerful source of strength for me. It has also shaped and inspired my attitudes around the work of crisis management. I have learned never to make the mistake of believing I am alone in any tough situation, and to always remember that together we are greater than the sum of our parts.

I have benefited from the opportunity to work at several organizations side by side with many tremendous leaders and teams, both in times of crisis response and on "blue-sky" days. To these people, I am eternally grateful. They gave me the opportunity – especially when I was young and inexperienced – to explore the world of crisis management, to get hands on, and they gave me the space to grow. Having the space to grow also meant that sometimes I would fail. Well, maybe, lots of times. I have learned from this example that there are days when the lessons come easily, and there are days when they don't. Either way, great leaders and great team members create the conditions where growth can happen – progress not perfection – this is what I have learned from the people who taught me best.

I also have to point out that this book was conceived of and written during the peak of the global COVID-19 pandemic. This was a historic global crisis that personally impacted every living person in the world in some way. For many, this has been a time of terrible suffering, loss, and difficulty. Yet once again, I was fortunate to stand side-by-side with friends and family who display unwavering strength of character, perseverance, patience, and grit. When times were at their worst no one among us could know what tomorrow would bring, or even sometimes what the next hours would bring. In those moments I saw the people around me – at work and at home – hold each other up, let each other shout or cry, and then simply do the next right thing. There were also of course moments of great joy which the pandemic could not extinguish: the birth of my youngest son, the celebrations of birthdays and holidays with our children, and the reunions with loved ones.

My sincere thanks to each of you:

Mom and Dad, Kathleen and Thomas Monahan, are my role models for grit and determination. They never told me that I needed to live life on life's terms. They showed me how it is done by the way they live their own lives. Then they gave me the freedom to figure it out and picked me up when I would fall. I will be lucky if I grow up to be half the man they showed me I could become. They also suffered through proofreading innumerable early drafts of this book. When they weren't doing that, they switched to Mema and Grandpa mode to look after the kids while the writing got done on weekends.

Bruce Blythe for making me believe writing a book about this was possible and for challenging me on why I hadn't gotten started on it already! Bruce has been a great source of support to me for many years, a true role model for crisis practitioners, and endlessly generous with his time and his ideas.

Dr. James Leflar for giving me inspiration in the early going, for his helpful feedback, and for showing me what it takes to write a book. His words kept me going at times when reaching the finish line just seemed too hard.

With sincere thanks and gratitude to David Lindstedt and Mark Armour for their support and for fearlessly pioneering ideas that meaningfully challenge traditional approaches.

Jordan Strauss for making so much time for me to talk through these ideas with him, and for his generous support in sharing his experience with me. Jordan is a titan in this field, and an extraordinary resource for anyone that has the opportunity to work with him.

Arjen Boin for his willingness to listen to these ideas and his intellectual generosity. Arjen is the leading thinker on crisis management among academics, and my hope is that his work continues to be reflected in our practice at the field.

Helena Parkinson, Julia Pollacco, Meredith Norwich, and the Editorial Team at Routledge.

My friends and colleagues who over the years have given me opportunities, busted down obstacles, patiently endured my whining, and put me in a place to succeed:

Ed Dickson, Larry Kunz, Nadya Babigian, Cody Beaver, Sharon Harris, Rich Reig, Lucia Aurello, Greg King, Shefali Kothari, Nick Santillo, Dave Leach, Rob Raffaele, Francis J. McCormick, Mark DeVoti, Mike Paszynsky, Russell Fischer, Andrew Peden and L5L Communications, Rachelle Loyear, and Mark Williams.

I would like to thank and acknowledge the reader for being open to the ideas contained here, and for being part of the solution. Thank you for the work you do. Because you do it well your efforts are often unacknowledged. But that does not diminish their significance. Even if one life is protected you have made a true difference.

Lastly and most of all, Libette who has seen me at my best and worst, through every crisis big and small since the beginning. None of it would be possible without you.

INDEX

Note: Page references in *italics* denote figures.

Printed in the United States
by Baker & Taylor Publisher Services